Jesus Says

"You Must Be Born Again"

Lawson Hanson

Note: Unless otherwise specified, the cited Bible text references are extracts from the KJV (King James Version, circa 1611) with updated, more modern spelling.

Contents

Chapter 1

Why listen to Jesus?

Jesus says: *"You must be born again."*

We will soon see where Jesus made this statement and discover the implications of these curious words.

By all accounts, from what we read in the Bible, Jesus was *"about thirty years of age"* when He came to the banks of the Jordan, to get baptized by John the Baptist:

> 16. *And Jesus, when he was baptized, went up straightway out of the water: and, lo, the heavens were opened unto him, and he saw the Spirit of God descending like a dove, and lighting upon him:*
> 17. *And lo a voice from heaven, saying, This is my beloved Son, in whom I am well pleased.*
> — Matthew 3:16–17

Notice that John the Baptist observed: *"the Spirit of God descending like a dove, and lighting upon him."*

We believe the anointed ministry of Jesus lasted for about three and a half years. During this time He went about doing good and working remarkable, wonderful miracles.

Of the noteworthy statements Jesus made and His wondrous deeds, the writers of the gospel books: *Matthew, Mark, Luke* and *John,* recorded what ever they could remember.

Jesus healed a man from leprosy; and healed a paralyzed man. He healed a woman who had an issue of blood for 12 years; all she did was *"touch the hem of His garment"* and Jesus said: *"thy faith hath made thee whole."*

Jesus healed a man with a withered hand; and two blind men. He healed a man who was dumb; another man who was both blind and dumb and another who was deaf and dumb.

Through the Holy Spirit, Jesus called upon God, the heavenly Father, to restore their health and limbs and their senses of sight and hearing and the ability to speak.

To the amazement of His disciples, Jesus walked on water and He calmed a great storm with His voice by speaking the words: *"Peace, be still."*

Jesus fed crowds of people who came out to hear Him teach. There was 5,000 and later another 4,000 people all fed from a few small loaves and little fishes.

Jesus healed all the people who came to Him to seek help and He even raised Lazarus and others, back to life, from the dead.

At times Jesus spoke *parables* to illustrate a point; often He gave us plain teaching and clear instruction, including commandments and guidance in righteous living.

In the closing verse of the gospel of John, the author writes:

> 25. *And there are also many other things which Jesus did, the which, if they should be written every one, I suppose that even the world itself could not contain the books that should be written. Amen.*
> — John 21:25

In the gospel of Matthew, at the start of chapter 17, we can read an account of when Jesus took with Him: *"Peter, James, and John his brother, and bringeth them up into an high mountain apart."*

While they were up there, the scriptures report:

> 5. ... *behold, a bright cloud overshadowed them: and behold a voice out of the cloud, which said, This is my beloved Son, in whom I am well pleased; hear ye him.*
> — Matthew 17:5

When the voice of Almighty God makes such a proclamation, how much attention should we give to His announcement: *"This is my beloved Son: in whom I am well pleased; hear ye him."*

It should be clear to us that every word Jesus speaks to us, both then and today, through what we can plainly read, recorded in the Bible, which is the written Word of God, is of significant importance.

What did God say? *"Hear ye him."* Take implicit notice of what Jesus says.

Given the four gospels and other books quoting what Jesus said, it could be reasonable for us to ask: *'Can we find any instruction that Jesus gave us that is of vital importance and is a life changing matter?'*

I believe the answer is a resounding *"Yes."*

For the last, almost fifty years of my life, I have been attending a church that preaches the gospel about God and His Son, Jesus Christ. You can find us here:

https://www.revivalcentres.org

I know this good news to be dependable and true.

I want to share the details with you, and anyone who will take the time to investigate this for themselves.

Either what I am writing is the truth, or it's false.

I believe you can verify the truth of this for yourself, within a matter of hours, or days, or weeks (as it took me).

Here is a useful starting point for the vital information Jesus shared:

> 1. *There was a man of the Pharisees, named Nicodemus, a ruler of the Jews:*
> 2. *The same came to Jesus by night, and said unto him, Rabbi, we know that thou art a teacher come from God: for no man can do these miracles that thou doest, except God be with him.*
> 3. *Jesus answered and said unto him, Verily, verily, I say unto thee, Except a man be born again, he cannot see the kingdom of God.*
> 4. *Nicodemus saith unto him, How can a man be born when he is old? can he enter the second time into his mother's womb, and be born?*
> 5. *Jesus answered, Verily, verily, I say unto thee, Except a man be born of water and of the Spirit, he cannot enter into the kingdom of God.*
> 6. *That which is born of the flesh is flesh; and that which is born of the Spirit is spirit.*
> 7. *Marvel not that I said unto thee, Ye must be born again.*
> — John 3:1–7

Look at the imperative phrase Jesus used: "*Ye must be born again.*"

That little word: "*must*" implies this is "*mandatory.*"

4

Without this, Jesus explained: *"Except a man be born again, he cannot see the kingdom of God"* and *"Except a man be born of water and of the Spirit, he cannot enter into the kingdom of God."*

In place of the two words: *"cannot see,"* substitute the phrase: *"cannot begin to comprehend."*

When we get *"born again"* it opens the eyes of our understanding and provides the way for us to gain entry into *"the kingdom of God."*

Nicodemus, an educated man, a Pharisee, didn't understand what Jesus meant; at that time.

The truth of the words Jesus spoke became clear on the day of Pentecost, about which we can read in the book of Acts, chapter 2, verses 1 to 4.

Before we do that, we need another piece of the information Jesus gave to His disciples, not long before He ascended up into heaven to be with Almighty God, the heavenly Father:

> 2. *Until the day in which he was taken up,*
> *after that he through the Holy Ghost had given*
> *commandments unto the apostles whom he had*
> *chosen:*
> 3. *To whom also he shewed himself alive after*
> *his passion by many infallible proofs, being seen*
> *of them forty days, and speaking of the things*
> *pertaining to the kingdom of God:*
> 4. *And, being assembled together with them,*
> *commanded them that they should not depart from*
> *Jerusalem, but wait for the promise of the Father,*
> *which, saith he, ye have heard of me.*
> 5. *For John truly baptized with water; but ye shall*
> *be baptized with the Holy Ghost not many days*
> *hence.*
> — Acts 1:2–5

The disciples did what Jesus *"commanded"* them in verse 4.

They gathered together and they *"waited"* in Jerusalem praying earnestly for the: *"promise of the Father"* that Jesus said would produce this experience: *"ye shall be baptized with the Holy Ghost."*

Not long after in the next chapter it reports:

> 1. *And when the day of Pentecost was fully come, they were all with one accord in one place.*
> 2. *And suddenly there came a sound from heaven as of a rushing mighty wind, and it filled all the house where they were sitting.*
> 3. *And there appeared unto them cloven tongues like as of fire, and it sat upon each of them.*
> 4. *And they were all filled with the Holy Ghost, and began to speak with other tongues, as the Spirit gave them utterance.*
> — Acts 2:1–4

The result of doing what Jesus commanded is: *"they were all filled with the Holy Ghost, and began to speak with other tongues, as the Spirit gave them utterance."* This is that *"promise of the Father"* through which they got changed like Jesus did as they became: *"baptized with the Holy Ghost."*

Remember the words Jesus spoke to the man named Nicodemus: *"Marvel not that I said unto thee, Ye must be born again."*

If we have seen those four verses at the start of Acts chapter 2 before, we might have thought: *"That was nice for the disciples."*

If we examine the surrounding verses we discover there were about 120 people gathered there. The disciples of Jesus were there and there were women, including Mary the mother of Jesus and his brethren, along with other believers. There is

6

reason to believe that Nicodemus could have been there too; I hope he was.

What happened next is even more miraculous.

By what we read, this out-pouring of God's Spirit was a noisy event and it roused the interest of those nearby.

One or two people scoffed at them and made light of the commotion. Most were curious to find out more.

Peter reminded them of a well-known passage from an Old Testament prophet named Joel, in which he had foretold the coming of this event.

> 12. *And they were all amazed, and were in doubt, saying one to another, What meaneth this?*
> 13. *Others mocking said, These men are full of new wine.*
> 14. *But Peter, standing up with the eleven, lifted up his voice, and said unto them, Ye men of Judaea, and all ye that dwell at Jerusalem, be this known unto you, and hearken to my words:*
> 15. *For these are not drunken, as ye suppose, seeing it is but the third hour of the day.*
> 16. *But this is that which was spoken by the prophet Joel;*
> 17. *And it shall come to pass in the last days, saith God, I will pour out of my Spirit upon all flesh: and your sons and your daughters shall prophesy, and your young men shall see visions, and your old men shall dream dreams:*
> 18. *And on my servants and on my handmaidens I will pour out in those days of my Spirit; and they shall prophesy:*
> 19. *And I will shew wonders in heaven above, and signs in the earth beneath; blood, and fire, and vapour of smoke:*
> 20. *The sun shall be turned into darkness, and the*

*moon into blood, before the great and notable day
of the Lord come:*
*21. And it shall come to pass, that whosoever shall
call on the name of the Lord shall be saved.*
— Acts 2:12–21

Look at verse 16. Peter knew the contemporary scriptures
and was well acquainted with the writings of their prophets.
Inspired by the Holy Spirit gift he had received with the
other believers moments before he was able to connect the
dots and state with certainty *"this is that which was spoken
by the prophet Joel"* and he quoted Joel's prophecy almost
word for word. See Joel chapter 2, verses 28 to 32.

Notice God says *"I will pour out my Spirit upon all flesh"*
and *"whosoever shall call on the name of the Lord shall be
saved."*

We do not get to *"demand"* anything from God.

He will respond to us when we *"call"* on Him with due
consideration and respect. We ask Him for the promised gift.

Peter laid the blame: *"whom ye have crucified,"* for the awful
abuse and agonizing death Jesus suffered, squarely at the feet
of the house of Israel:

*36. Therefore let all the house of Israel know
assuredly, that God hath made the same Jesus,
whom ye have crucified, both Lord and Christ.*
*37. Now when they heard this, they were pricked
in their heart, and said unto Peter and to the rest
of the apostles, Men and brethren, what shall we
do?*
*38. Then Peter said unto them, Repent, and be
baptized every one of you in the name of Jesus
Christ for the remission of sins, and ye shall
receive the gift of the Holy Ghost.*

39. *For the promise is unto you, and to your children, and to all that are afar off, even as many as the LORD our God shall call.*
— Acts 2:36–39

The crowd was attentive and their remorse prompted them to ask the question: *"What shall we do?"*

Peter's response in verses 38 and 39 (read them again) was precisely what they needed to hear. In verse 41 we read this:

41. *Then they that gladly received his word were baptized: and the same day there were added unto them about three thousand souls.*
— Acts 2:41

Peter's advice worked for about 3,000 people on that day.

That initial 3,120 people was not the end of the matter. The last sentence in Acts chapter 2, verse 47, reads:

"And the Lord added to the church daily such as should be saved."

There are other sections of the New Testament that describe God's continuous and ongoing presentation of this special gift called: *"the promise of the Father"* to *"whosoever shall call on the name of the Lord."*

My favourite is where this same man, Peter the apostle, got called by God to go and preach to the house of Cornelius. This man Cornelius was a Roman centurion, he was not a man from the house of Israel.

In those days they considered it *"unlawful"* for a Jew to enter the house of anyone from another nation. You should read the entire fascinating story.

See the whole of Acts chapter 10, and then Acts chapter 11, verses 1 to 18.

Here is a small excerpt from chapter 10:

> 44. *While Peter yet spake these words, the Holy Ghost fell on all them which heard the word.*
> 45. *And they of the circumcision which believed were astonished, as many as came with Peter, because that on the Gentiles also was poured out the gift of the Holy Ghost.*
> 46. *For they heard them speak with tongues, and magnify God. Then answered Peter,*
> 47. *Can any man forbid water, that these should not be baptized, which have received the Holy Ghost as well as we?*
> — Acts 10:44–47

How did they all *know* that *"on the Gentiles also was poured out the gift of the Holy Ghost?"*

This: *"For they heard them speak with tongues, and magnify God."*

The evidence is audible, for all to hear.

This tells us the other Jews who had accompanied Peter: *"were astonished."* It seems they thought this experience was theirs alone.

Almighty God has other, far reaching plans.

When Peter returned to Jerusalem, after preaching to Cornelius, he got called to give an account of his contentious actions; he used these words:

> 15. *And as I began to speak, the Holy Ghost fell on them, as on us at the beginning.*

16. *Then remembered I the word of the Lord, how
that he said, John indeed baptized with water; but
ye shall be baptized with the Holy Ghost.*
17. *Forasmuch then as God gave them the like gift
as he did unto us, who believed on the Lord Jesus
Christ; what was I, that I could withstand God?*
18. *When they heard these things, they held their
peace, and glorified God, saying, Then hath God
also to the Gentiles granted repentance unto life.*
— Acts 11:15–18

Peter said: *"God gave them the like gift as he did unto us."*
That little word: *"like"* got translated from the Greek word
"isos" from which we derive the term *"Isosceles"* (as in a
triangle with two *"equal"* sides and two *"equal"* angles).

Peter said: *"God gave them the 'equal' gift."*

Those who had at first contended with Peter about his
preaching to Cornelius accepted that: *"Then hath God also
to the Gentiles granted repentance unto life."*

This *"promise of the Father"* is available to anyone,
anywhere.

The good news is that Peter's advice from Acts chapter 2,
verse 38, *still works today.*

All we need to do is follow Peter's instructions, *to the letter.*

That is, we must do this: *Repent, and be baptized every one
of you in the name of Jesus Christ for the remission of sins,
and ye shall receive the gift of the Holy Ghost.*

The term *"Repent"* comes from a Greek word that means
"with a change of knowing."

We need to allow ourself to have a *change* of thinking.

We might need to forget *what we think we know* about
God, or could need to reconsider what we got taught by

11

misinformed religionists.

For example, a never ending cycle of doing the wrong thing and going to confession each week; then doing what we know is wrong again and repeating that process, over and over and over again, makes little sense. That practise derived from an Old Testament way of thinking.

Consider this verse from the prophet Isaiah:

> 13. *Bring no more vain oblations; incense is an abomination unto me; the new moons and sabbaths, the calling of assemblies, I cannot away with; it is iniquity, even the solemn meeting.*
> — Isaiah 1:13

We were incapable of keeping the Old Testament regulations. God had become weary of our lack lustre attempts.

That is not what God and Jesus want from us today.

The Psalmist knew what God wants:

> 17. *The sacrifices of God are a broken spirit: a broken and a contrite heart, O God, thou wilt not despise.*
> — Psalms 51:17

God wants us to admit defeat. We can not do everything on our own. God wants us to approach Him from a humble and repentant state of mind.

We have grown so far away from understanding God's ways.

Through God's grace we can make progress in the right direction.

The Holy Spirit *"born again"* experience sets us free. We can refrain from doing wrong at *all* times now.

The church I attend burns no incense, and the general meetings we hold are never solemn affairs. We always have happy and bright singing; bringing praises to God.

We believe God approves of what we attempt to do because He upholds the gospel message we preach with the *"signs following"* evidence He promised to send.

God provides a free *"gift"* that Jesus called *"the promise of the Father"* and this transcends those old ways of thinking.

We might need to straighten out our lives and actions to conform to the way we know God wants us to be:

> 8. *He hath shewed thee, O man, what is good; and what doth the LORD require of thee, but to do justly, and to love mercy, and to walk humbly with thy God?*
> — Micah 6:8

From my experience, this does not hurt. Try it. We can start to feel good about ourself. Show mercy to others; do not seek revenge. Jesus says we should turn the other cheek, and forgive people who do any wrong to us.

I expect you'll find they do not know about the grace and mercy of God.

Preach the gospel to them. That could help.

We are God's creation; not the other way around.

Don't shout at God. He can hear you.
Don't curse and swear. He will turn away.

We need to approach God in a circumspect manner with heart felt honesty and humility; a state of repentance where we want to find the truth.

We need to believe what Jesus plainly tells us:

"Ye must be born again."

It's a three step process:

1. **Repent**

Turn aside from doing your own thing all the time.

Make a humble and honest approach towards God.

2. **Get baptized**

Do what God has asked us to do.

Go through the short process of water baptism.

It takes a little bit of humility.

It demonstrates our intentions are good.

The Bible says *"all have sinned and come short of the glory of God."*

Jesus died to wash away our sins.

3. **Receive God's Holy Spirit**

Ask God for the promise of the Father.

Spend time talking to God with humility and sincerity.

We will know the moment we receive the *"promise of the Father"* because we will start speaking in an unlearned tongue.

If this takes a little while, do not get discouraged.

Ask and keep on asking. Jesus says:

> 7. *Ask, and it shall be given you; seek, and ye shall find; knock, and it shall be opened unto you:*
> 8. *For every one that asketh receiveth; and he that seeketh findeth; and to him that knocketh it shall be opened.*
> — Matthew 7:7–8

Before long we expect there will be a pleasant surprise.

Chapter 2

Miracles from God

When I was 25 years old, a student who was completing his Ph.D work at the University of Melbourne told me about his *"born again"* experience in 1975.

It took me about five or six months to pluck up the courage to accept his invitations to attend a meeting at the church he went to. I am so glad I did.

It felt as if I was coming home! It's a happy place with a sea of genuine smiling faces. I got baptized after my second meeting. For the first time in over a decade I felt as if I had taken a step in the right direction — towards God instead of always moving the other way.

Five weeks after I got baptized, in the manner that John the Baptist used, by complete immersion in water, I received my own *"day of Pentecost"* experience.

I received the gift of the Holy Spirit. I was speaking in other tongues as the Spirit gave me the utterance. My speech was quiet, yet clear.

This audible gift gives us a personal prayer language that gets used for our direct communication with Almighty God. It's a precious gift that He expects us to use every day. It brings great benefits including peace and comfort and joy. It provides Spiritual insight into the kingdom of God.

Speaking to His disciples, Jesus used these words to talk about this gift He also called: *"the Comforter"* and *"the Spirit of truth"*:

> 7. *Nevertheless I tell you the truth; It is expedient for you that I go away: for if I go not away, the Comforter will not come unto you; but if I depart, I will send him unto you.*
>
> ...
>
> 13. *Howbeit when he, the Spirit of truth, is come, he will guide you into all truth: for he shall not speak of himself; but whatsoever he shall hear, that shall he speak: and he will shew you things to come.*
> 14. *He shall glorify me: for he shall receive of mine, and shall shew it unto you.*
> — John 16:7, 13 and 14

In a split second, on the 27th July, 1975, I knew for certain that God is real and that He loves me more than I can imagine. There's One God who *can* answer our call. He says He will.

Everything in those scripture verses we read is true, beyond any shadow of a doubt. I believe and know that I am, by His grace, adopted into God's heavenly family. The same exceptional position is waiting for you:

> 14. *For as many as are led by the Spirit of God, they are the sons of God.*
> 15. *For ye have not received the spirit of bondage again to fear; but ye have received the Spirit of adoption, whereby we cry, Abba, Father.*
> — Romans 8: 14–15

Almighty God is God of all creation. He and His Son, Jesus Christ, have provided a way for us to receive the gift of the Holy Spirit. This provides us with our own evidence of the absolute veracity of God and His Word.

God's promised gift is for everyone, every where.

There's *nothing* better. Please ask God to give you His precious gift.

During the five weeks between when I got baptized, on Sunday the 22nd June, 1975, and when subsequent to that, I then received the gift of the Holy Spirit, on Sunday 27th July, 1975, I experienced my own remarkable, *personal* miracles from God.

One evening I attended a smaller, mid-week, *"house meeting"* where all I remember hearing is: *"God is a healing God."* Near the end of that meeting, during a brief time of prayer, I raised my hand to get one of the elders to pray for me. I asked for prayer that God would heal my nose. It had been in pain for about one whole year after I got punched in the face during a bit of a fight.

The person who prayed for me said these simple words: *"Thank you God for healing this man's nose"* followed by a couple of: *"Hallelujah,"* *"Praise the Lord,"* *"Hallelujah"* and *"Bless Your wonderful Name, thank You Jesus"* words of prayer and giving of thanks to God. Soon after that I went home.

During the night I woke up feeling rather warm and there was a tingling sensation in the middle of my face. It felt as if my nose was getting manipulated around and around in a gentle circular motion.

I got up to check there was nobody else there. I lived alone. In the middle of winter in Melbourne, I soon cooled down. Then I went back to bed and slept soundly. In the morning there was another new sensation: No more pain! Wow.

Healed over night. Thank you Lord.

At another small house meeting in the next week or two I heard: *"God can do anything!"* I took it upon myself to say to God: *"Okay God. If you can do anything: Stop me from smoking."* Almost a challenge. I do not think I even remembered to say: *"Please."* I am sorry Lord.

Later that night, after I got home from the meeting, I went to light up a cigarette before heading off to bed. At that time I was already a chain smoker — over 30 each day.

That cigarette tasted awful; horrible; foul. In despair, I opened a new carton of cigarettes, took out a fresh pack and tried to light up another cigarette, discovering that the *new* one tasted awful, too.

In disbelief (almost) I went to bed and slept soundly until the next morning. When I awoke I tried to light up another cigarette. It tasted disgusting!

Then I realised that God enabled me to quit smoking — *overnight*.

All my praises go to God.

If you have ever been a smoker you will understand how difficult is the act of giving up that addiction to nicotine. I had at previous times tried quitting by myself and had always failed within a day or two at most.

Since that day (about 50 years ago now) I have never had the craving for another cigarette; in fact even the slightest smell of cigarette smoke makes me feel ill. It always serves as a good reminder about this miracle God performed for me, even *before* I was *"born again."*

One day during those first five weeks the desire to drink alcohol deserted me. In truth, I was a borderline alcoholic. I was taking strong drink almost every day — always unable to refrain.

I had the sudden urge to pour my small collection of beer and wines and spirits down the sink. I lined up the bottles and I did. It felt most *liberating.*

Since doing that I have never wanted to touch another glass of beer or wine or alcohol of any kind.

I noticed another miracle: my speech was beginning to contain less and less profanities and expletives. I could almost string together a couple of sentences without the need for any of those vulgar, objectionable terms.

Rude words are meaningless noise! Leave them out.

Overjoyed by these personal miracles and the fact that my senses of taste and smell were starting to return so soon after I had stopped smoking. These miracles coupled with the realisation that I was sleeping soundly *every* night instead of tossing and turning half awake for hours on end as I had been before.

I was at home, praying by myself saying words like: *"Hallelujah"* and small phrases like: *"Praise the Lord"* and *"Thank you Lord."* In my mind I was asking God for the promise of the Father, the Holy Spirit.

I was thanking God as I was thinking about those remarkable miracles He had already performed for me.

After a short space of time, while giving God thanks and repeating those two or three words of prayer I had learned, I realised I had actually received the gift of the Holy Spirit.

How did I know? I was speaking in other tongues. It was quiet, yet clear, an unmistakable change. The words streamed out of my mouth. There was no extraordinary effort required.

I could stop the praying in tongues and I could start praying in tongues again. I was in complete control of this wonderful gift that God had graciously bestowed upon me.

It felt wonderful and I kept praying for a little while longer listening to those unknown words. A scripture I had heard three or four days earlier came to mind:

> 14. *For if I pray in an unknown tongue, my spirit prayeth, but my understanding is unfruitful.*
> — 1 Corinthians 14:14

I realised that I was able to do what God wanted:

> 24. *God is a Spirit: and they that worship him must worship him in spirit and in truth.*
> — John 4:24

I realised that miracles still *do* happen today. The God of all creation has never changed.

The Old Testament declares this:

> 6. *For I am the LORD, I change not; therefore ye sons of Jacob are not consumed.*
> — Malachi 3:6

The New Testament declares:

> 8. *Jesus Christ the same yesterday, and to day, and for ever.*
> — Hebrews 13:8

These promises in God's Word mean that when people receive God's promised gift of the Holy Ghost today, they will have the same experience that I had. This is the *same* experience that more than 3,000 people had on the day of Pentecost, about 2,000 years ago.

Since *that* day of Pentecost, this experience, a miracle from God, is *always* accompanied by clear audible evidence, that is: *"speaking with unlearned tongues."*

It's an unmistakable gift from God. There's no way we can fake it. God provides the words for us to speak to Him.

For anyone who *tries* to make up their own words of gibberish for themselves; please remember: It's *impossible* to fool God.

Consider these words:

> 12. *For the word of God is quick, and powerful, and sharper than any twoedged sword, piercing even to the dividing asunder of soul and spirit, and of the joints and marrow, and is a discerner of the thoughts and intents of the heart.*
> 13. *Neither is there any creature that is not manifest in his sight: but all things are naked and opened unto the eyes of him with whom we have to do.*
> — Hebrews 4:12–13

God knows our every thought. He knows our heart felt intentions. It's impossible to hide *anything* from God.

We will know within our inner-most being when God has made us to become *"born again"* through the baptism of the Holy Spirit.

The evidence of this miraculous in-filling of the *"promise of the Father"* is audible, for all to hear. You will know and those around you will know. Tangible, undeniable evidence, within and without.

God has promised us:

> 3. *Call unto me, and I will answer thee, and shew*

*thee great and mighty things, which thou knowest
not.*
— Jeremiah 33:3

I praise God for His ever merciful grace and the extent of
His wonderful plan of salvation. Given to every person, every
where.

To gain access we need to read His Word, and agree to His
conditions.

What conditions? The condensed version of those is
contained within the statement Peter made in answer to the
question: *"What shall we do?"*

*"Repent, and be baptized every one of you in the name of
Jesus Christ for the remission of sins, and ye shall receive
the gift of the Holy Ghost."*

What does that mean?

The Bible says this:

> 23. *For all have sinned, and come short of the
> glory of God;*
> — Romans 3:23

In our natural human state we fall short of what God expects
of us.

The prophet Jeremiah got inspired to write these words of
warning and encouragement:

> 9. *The heart is deceitful above all things, and
> desperately wicked: who can know it?*
> 10. *I the LORD search the heart, I try the reins,
> even to give every man according to his ways, and
> according to the fruit of his doings.*
> — Jeremiah 17:9–10

From Bible history we understand that God placed Adam and Eve in the Garden of Eden; a beautiful place of His creation:

> 8. *And the LORD God planted a garden eastward in Eden; and there he put the man whom he had formed.*
> 9. *And out of the ground made the LORD God to grow every tree that is pleasant to the sight, and good for food; the tree of life also in the midst of the garden, and the tree of knowledge of good and evil.*
> — Genesis 2:8–9

God was there with them when they walked and talked with Him:

> 16. *And the LORD God commanded the man, saying, Of every tree of the garden thou mayest freely eat:*
> 17. *But of the tree of the knowledge of good and evil, thou shalt not eat of it: for in the day that thou eatest thereof thou shalt surely die.*
> — Genesis 2:16–17

There was one life and death condition that Adam chose to break; or couldn't be bothered to keep. I expect you have read the story.

Since that time most of the human race remained separated from God.

God is a Spirit, and the conditions are non-negotiable.

God through His Spirit has devised a wonderful plan of Salvation.

God sent His own Son, Jesus Christ, into the world to pay the awful price for our sins and make the way back for us.

Jesus got born with a human body like us. The Bible says He got tempted like us, and yet, He did not sin.

A miraculous change happened to Jesus when He got baptized, as we read in Matthew chapter 3, back in my opening paragraphs.

The book of John has this to say about where John the Baptist operated:

> 23. *And John also was baptizing in Aenon near to Salim, because there was much water there: and they came, and were baptized.*
> — John 3:23

The important point: *"there was much water there."*

Baptism involves a complete covering over with the water. This is symbolic of burying our old ungodly life — for good.

It's not a token sprinkling when we are babies who are too young to know what the activity means.

Getting baptized is an action we must take when we reach an age of understanding and can know what we are doing.

In these verses from 1st Peter, chapter 3, we find that our baptism is symbolic of a separation from our old lifestyle. It demonstrates that we have *"a good conscience toward God:"*

> 18. *For Christ also hath once suffered for sins, the just for the unjust, that he might bring us to God, being put to death in the flesh, but quickened by the Spirit:*
> 19. *By which also he went and preached unto the spirits in prison;*

20. Which sometime were disobedient, when once the longsuffering of God waited in the days of Noah, while the ark was a preparing, wherein few, that is, eight souls were saved by water.
21. The like figure whereunto even baptism doth also now save us (not the putting away of the filth of the flesh, but the answer of a good conscience toward God,) by the resurrection of Jesus Christ:
22. Who is gone into heaven, and is on the right hand of God; angels and authorities and powers being made subject unto him.
— 1 Peter 3:18–22

The words in verse 21 say that our baptism in water shows *"the answer of a good conscience toward God."*

It's like Noah and his family who needed to take time building an ark made of gopher wood and build it according to the commandment of God; a certain length and breadth and height with specified levels or decks and with rooms that God described in much detail.

Their years of dedicated toil showed they were steadfast toward God and His command.

After its completion then God brought forty days and forty nights of rains to cover the Earth and separate them from the rest of the world who chose not to acknowledge or yield to God.

Today, if we will agree to remove ourself from our old ways of life, the sin and separation from God, showing our sincerity by getting baptized in water, then Jesus Christ promises that He and the heavenly Father, will come and make their *"abode"* with us:

23. Jesus answered and said unto him, If a man love me, he will keep my words: and my Father

25

will love him, and we will come unto him, and
make our abode with him.
— John 14:23

Through *"the promise of the Father"* we come full circle and
return to life like Adam and Eve enjoyed in the garden of
Eden. We now walk and talk with the Spirit of God and with
Jesus Christ — every day.

I am so glad I listened to the Ph.D student in 1975, who was
eager to share the gospel message with me, and anyone else
who would listen.

Thank you Martin, for your dedication in preaching the
Word of God to me and the whomsoever. Thank you for
the patience you had when trying to encourage me to get
to a meeting to let me find out the truth for myself. Sincere
thanks to a dear friend who has become: Pastor Martin.

As brothers in the Lord, we praise and thank God and Jesus
Christ for the wonderful plan of salvation and for providing
us with the opportunity to get adopted into God's family —
giving us the hope and expectation that we will live forever
with Them.

I apologize for taking so long in getting a pen to paper for
my attempt to spread this wonderful life changing news.

Chapter 3

Fruit of the Spirit

From this point on we will look at what a *"born again"* Spirit-filled person can expect *after* they have received *"the gift of the Father"* and can now speak in other tongues.

Please go back and read my first chapter if you have not yet reached that goal. Do what Peter instructed when he answered the question *"What shall we do?"*

There's a host of verses in the scriptures that mention the wonderful benefits we gain from receiving the gift of the Holy Ghost.

For example, in the book of Galatians, chapter 5, we find the in-filling of the Holy Spirit provides each of us with a set of nine amazing attributes, instantly available for our day to day and moment by moment use.

Here is the verses describing these and our new perspective:

> 22. *But the fruit of the Spirit is love, joy, peace, longsuffering, gentleness, goodness, faith,*
> 23. *Meekness, temperance: against such there is no law.*
> 24. *And they that are Christ's have crucified the*

flesh with the affections and lusts.
25. If we live in the Spirit, let us also walk in the
Spirit.
— Galatians 5: 22–25

Look at those nine exquisite characteristics or behavioural expressions listed in verses 22 and 23.

This is part of the gift of the Holy Spirit.

Verses 24 and 25 show the new context in which we now exist. We are people who must *"walk in the Spirit"* because we now *"live in the Spirit"* and we have *"crucified"* or done away with all yearning for the unrestrained and wanton ways of the world.

It's no longer us alone with our own abilities. We are now anointed, like Jesus Christ, baptized with the Holy Ghost. The Spirit of the Living God resides within us. The fruit of the Spirit is become an integral part of us.

A verse in 2nd Corinthians, chapter 5 reminds us that now:

7. For we walk by faith, not by sight:
— 2 Corinthians 5:7

It doesn't matter how bad our circumstances appear, illness and difficulties can look insurmountable. We know God exists, beyond any shadow of doubt. We know He loves us and cares for us and He hears and answers our prayers. We keep looking to Him, not at the problems, asking God and Jesus Christ to help us overcome.

We can apply each of those wonderful characteristics or identifying *"fruit of the Holy Spirit"* attributes of our new *"born again"* self in every situation we will face in life.

These help us to maintain a cool, calm and collected frame of mind and we will find it easy to remain at peace and steadfast in the faith.

I hope it could help to take a closer inspection of that list of the nine *"fruit of the Spirit:"*

1. **love**

Jesus says:

> 15. *If ye love me, keep my commandments.*
> — John 14:15

We do what God commands.

Exercising this *"fruit of the Spirit"* towards others helps us to spread the gospel message, guiding people with the words Jesus spoke: *"Ye must be born again."*

2. **joy**

Jesus says:

> 10. *If ye keep my commandments, ye shall abide in my love; even as I have kept my Father's commandments, and abide in his love.*
> 11. *These things have I spoken unto you, that my joy might remain in you, and that your joy might be full.*
> — John 15:10–11

We have a joyous life. Yes, there can still be momentary afflictions. In general, there is exceeding joy. We now know God on a personal basis. That brings me a great amount of joy every day.

3. **peace**

Here is what Jesus says:

> 26. *But the Comforter, which is the Holy Ghost, whom the Father will send in my name, he shall teach you all things, and bring all things to your remembrance, whatsoever I have said unto you.*
> 27. *Peace I leave with you, my peace I give unto you: not as the world giveth, give I unto you. Let not your heart be troubled, neither let it be afraid.*
> — John 14: 26–27

The Holy Ghost experience is one of the most peaceful and comforting of all experiences I know. In this world of turmoil and strife, we have no need to feel troubled of fearful. The thought of dying is no longer a concern.

4. **longsuffering**

This verse from 2nd Peter came to mind:

> 9. *The Lord is not slack concerning his promise, as some men count slackness; but is longsuffering to us-ward, not willing that any should perish, but that all should come to repentance.*
> — 2 Peter 3:9

Not something we need to *"suffer,"* but rather, giving us the ability to exercise continuous patience.

Verse 9 says the Lord is longsuffering towards us, giving us all the opportunity to repent.

We can exercise longsuffering toward family and friends, who for reasons unknown, do not jump at the gospel we preach.

We do not get upset with them. We ask the Lord to show us other words we can say to them to help them see.

We do not badger people continually. There's a scripture that says *"Here a little; there a little."* Not everyone can accept what we have to say in one sitting. For example, it took me six months — I was slow!

5. **gentleness**

This verse in James chapter 3 encourages us to be wise, treat people with gentleness:

> 17. *But the wisdom that is from above is*
> *first pure, then peaceable, gentle, and easy*
> *to be intreated, full of mercy and good fruits,*
> *without partiality, and without hypocrisy.*
> — James 3:17

We have received the utmost ability to remain composed and in quiet control of ourself. Our interaction with others should get based upon the same way God's wisdom, from above, treats us.

It's a tall order to fill on our own. These nine precious fruit of the Holy Spirit we have inherited will help us to do what is required. They show us how much care God has for His creation.

6. **goodness**

These delightful words about goodness, come from the book of Psalms, chapter 23:

> 6. *Surely goodness and mercy shall follow me*
> *all the days of my life: and I will dwell in the*
> *house of the LORD for ever.*
> — Psalms 23:6

This God-given ability helps us have nothing but the best of intentions at heart in our interaction with others and to carry those through by the goodness and mercy that God has shown toward us.

7. faith

God, in His wisdom has given us *"faith,"* as another one of these magnificent fruit of the Spirit.

Because we have received the evidence-based *"promise of the Father"* our *"faith"* is now in-built.

One of my favourite verses about *"faith"* is this:

> 5. *That your faith should not stand in the wisdom of men, but in the power of God.*
> — 1 Corinthians 2:5

Our faith does not *"stand"* or need to get *constructed* by the wisdom of men, rather, through the undeniable born again evidence we have now received it stands all by itself *"in the power of God."*

8. meekness

Meekness is the ability to remain in full control of our emotions instead of being on the offensive all the time.

Writing to the Ephesians, the apostle Paul had this to say as he reminded them of the necessity for meekness:

> 1. *I therefore, the prisoner of the Lord, beseech you that ye walk worthy of the vocation wherewith ye are called,*
> 2. *With all lowliness and meekness, with longsuffering, forbearing one another in love;*
> 3. *Endeavouring to keep the unity of the Spirit in the bond of peace.*
> — Ephesians 4: 1–3

Walk worthy of the vocation: stay humble, stay meek, stay patient.

9. temperance

Simon Peter wrote the following beautiful words to summarize much of our expectation for being faithful, virtuous and knowledgeable, acting with temperance and exercising patience, godliness, brotherly kindness and charity:

> 2. *Grace and peace be multiplied unto you through the knowledge of God, and of Jesus our Lord,*
> 3. *According as his divine power hath given unto us all things that pertain unto life and godliness, through the knowledge of him that hath called us to glory and virtue:*
> 4. *Whereby are given unto us exceeding great and precious promises: that by these ye might be partakers of the divine nature, having escaped the corruption that is in the world through lust.*
> 5. *And beside this, giving all diligence, add to your faith virtue; and to virtue knowledge;*
> 6. *And to knowledge temperance; and to temperance patience; and to patience godliness;*
> 7. *And to godliness brotherly kindness; and to brotherly kindness charity.*
> 8. *For if these things be in you, and abound, they make you that ye shall neither be barren nor unfruitful in the knowledge of our Lord Jesus Christ.*
> — 2 Peter 1: 2–8

A term we seldom hear in society these days, *"temperance"* describes our ability to be considerate,

33

impartial, level headed and moderate; staying in self control, sober minded, self disciplined and acting with self restraint.

God, in His boundless grace and mercy toward us has poured out of His Spirit upon all flesh, as promised in the words of the prophet Joel. See: Joel chapter 2, verses 28 and 29.

God knows how difficult life has become, yet He expects more from us. We are His creation, in whom He has placed enormous potential.

We no longer need to feel trapped, in the strife which surrounds us in life; the so-called *"works of the flesh."*

Receiving the comprehensive *"born again"* gift from God provides us with *"the measure of the faith"* and all the other attributes we need:

> 3. *For I say, through the grace given unto me, to every man that is among you, not to think of himself more highly than he ought to think; but to think soberly, according as God hath dealt to every man the measure of faith.*
> — Romans 12:3

We need to *"believe"* that this is our new *"born again"* state of being.

These attributes get given to us by God. They are none of our own doing. Remembering to apply and exercise these God given *"fruit of the Spirit"* is part of maintaining our state of repentance and humility before God.

We should endeavour to preserve this new sense of thinking, now that we know God and how much He cares for us.

Don't let go of this repentance. This change to our understanding. We must hang on to this new-found way of thinking with all the determination and might we can muster. God will help us do that.

Call upon God when the going gets tough. Remember to pray in tongues often. Use His precious gift. It does not need to be at the top of our voice. We talk to God. Don't shout. God is not deaf. His hearing extends across the entire universe.

In 1st Peter we find these words of both exhortation and warning:

> 6. *Humble yourselves therefore under the mighty hand of God, that he may exalt you in due time:*
> 7. *Casting all your care upon him; for he careth for you.*
> 8. *Be sober, be vigilant; because your adversary the devil, as a roaring lion, walketh about, seeking whom he may devour:*
> 9. *Whom resist stedfast in the faith, knowing that the same afflictions are accomplished in your brethren that are in the world.*
> 10. *But the God of all grace, who hath called us unto his eternal glory by Christ Jesus, after that ye have suffered a while, make you perfect, stablish, strengthen, settle you.*
> 11. *To him be glory and dominion for ever and ever. Amen.*
> — 1 Peter 5:6–11

God will help us overcome, if we will make a stand.

Smoking, drinking, gambling, riotous living, endless partying, taking illicit drugs and other associated activities, should all become fading memories of our receding and distant past.

We have no need to ever be involved in any of that again. Don't even think about it!

God is not trying to make life difficult for us. To the contrary, He advises us that He has now equipped us with all we need to be able to rise above the ungodly features of our prior existence in the world.

Most people I know who had turned to alcohol or drugs, or both, did so in the hopes that they could escape the reality of their world, in which they found no satisfying answers. They hoped they could get away from, or at least try to drown or deaden or forget their sorrows for a while.

I know, years ago, I was there myself. Now, I can assure anyone, that the answers provided directly by Almighty God, will far surpass any momentary relief we may find at the bottom of a bottle.

Do what Jesus commands: *"Ye must be born again."*

We experience that by following the instructions that Peter the apostle gave to the crowd of onlookers on the day of Pentecost. See: Acts, chapter 2, verses 38 and 39.

I praise and thank our wonderful God every day, because I prefer to rejoice over everything in which He helps me take the necessary control over my own actions, thoughts and emotions.

God can remove our addictions. God helps us overcome every temptation. All we need do is *"Ask, in faith."*

Remember to believe that for God, *"nothing shall be impossible."* He can do more than we ask or think.

Look at the beautiful words in these verses:

> 20. *Now unto him that is able to do exceeding abundantly above all that we ask or think, according to the power that worketh in us,*
> 21. *Unto him be glory in the church by Christ Jesus throughout all ages, world without end. Amen.*

— Ephesians 3:20–21

Through the application of these nine *"born again"* fruit of the Spirit in our life the living gets better as we make use of them. We can expect God to work in ways that: *"do exceeding abundantly above all that we ask or think."*

Chapter 4

The voice gifts

If you have attended any meetings in a church where all
the members are *"born again"* Christians, each one able to
"speak in other tongues," then I hope you will have heard the
operation of what is commonly called: *"the voice gifts of the
Holy Spirit."*

Our church operates these straight after the *"Communion"*
part of our meetings; before we invite anyone to come out
into the aisles for prayer, if they have any need for healing, or
are seeking to receive the Holy Ghost.

Listen up. This is the time when God speaks to His people.
He has chosen this method to speak to us about His ways,
His will, His plan, His purpose.

God reminds us about His expectations and our
responsibilities. He reminds us of His mercy and His grace
towards us and the great and precious promises He has made.
He exhorts us to call upon Him while He is near and to keep
on making a stand for the faith.

The first time we hear these voice gifts of the Holy Spirit
there can be questions in our mind about how, who, when,
where and what that all means.

Let's take a look.

In the same way the *"fruit of the Spirit"* is a composite part of the wonderful gift that God gives us and we *all* have access to those nine *"fruit,"* so too, is another nine miraculous features called the *"spiritual gifts."* We will look at all of them in more detail in my next chapter.

Here I wanted to concentrate on three of the gifts. These are *"tongues," "interpretation of tongues"* and *"prophecy."*

Why? Because it is these three we observe in operation during most meetings of the church. I hope the following detail can help us see how much God cares about us and the way He expects us to use these miracle components of the precious gift He has given.

The opening verses in 1st Corinthians, chapter 1, tell us this long letter came from Paul. Here he is writing to the church at Corinth:

> 1. *Paul called to be an apostle of Jesus Christ through the will of God, and Sosthenes our brother,*
> 2. *Unto the church of God which is at Corinth, to them that are sanctified in Christ Jesus, called to be saints, with all that in every place call upon the name of Jesus Christ our Lord, both their's and ours:*
> 3. *Grace be unto you, and peace, from God our Father, and from the Lord Jesus Christ.*
> — 1 Corinthians 1:1–3

When next we read words from chapter 14, we will know who is speaking or writing to *"the church of God"* in which we are now a functioning part.

Paul covers these three *"voice gifts"* in considerable detail and he provides sound advice on how best to operate these audible gifts in the church.

If reading what I have written below gets to be too much of a struggle, I suggest setting it aside for a day or two and coming back when you have had time to rest and refresh your mind through praying and talking to God with your new unlearned tongue.

Let's read what Paul wrote:

1. *Follow after charity, and desire spiritual gifts, but rather that ye may prophesy.*
2. *For he that speaketh in an unknown tongue speaketh not unto men, but unto God: for no man understandeth him; howbeit in the spirit he speaketh mysteries.*
3. *But he that prophesieth speaketh unto men to edification, and exhortation, and comfort.*
4. *He that speaketh in an unknown tongue edifieth himself; but he that prophesieth edifieth the church.*
5. *I would that ye all spake with tongues but rather that ye prophesied: for greater is he that prophesieth than he that speaketh with tongues, except he interpret, that the church may receive edifying.*
— 1 Corinthians 14: 1–5

He starts by reminding us that we should: *"follow after charity."* We must exhibit *"the love of God,"* about which he wrote in his earlier chapter 13.

Why is this important?

In a large auditorium or gathering of the church it can be difficult to hear when another person starts to operate one of these vocal gifts.

If we have started speaking and we hear another person start speaking too, it is likely they did not hear us.

The charitable thing for us to do is for us to stop. Our turn will come again. Do not take offense. God will bless us for our humility.

Paul exhorts that we should also *"desire spiritual gifts, but rather"* or in particular, that we should seek to use the gift of *"prophecy."*

Why is that important?

Speaking in our natural language as we do when giving a message of *"prophecy"* can serve to *"edify"* or encourage the church as a whole; provided of course that we are listening.

Look at the first clause in verse 2: *"For he that speaketh in an unknown tongue speaketh not unto men, but unto God."*

Know this: Speaking in other tongues *is* speaking to God.

In the other verses Paul explains that no man understands us when we speak in an *"unknown"* tongue. His advice to us is that we should *"desire"* to make use of the gifts of *"interpretation of tongues"* and *"prophecy."*

Spirit filled Christians have the ability to speak in other tongues fluently, like we speak in our native tongue.

God understands what we say in other tongues. At most times people do not understand those words.

Because we now have the ability to pray in other tongues, we can all be potential candidates to speak a short message in tongues when the pastor says it's time for that part of the meeting.

If you are like me, you may get off to a false start once or twice before it becomes more natural. Don't get embarrassed. Those around you will get excited because you have taken such a step in faith.

When our operation of that gift of the Spirit is comfortable in us, we can and should ask God to let us use these other two voice gifts. Because these will help to *"edify"* or bring greater benefit to the church.

In the next eight verses, Paul explains reasoning and guidelines, through his use of descriptive analogies of audible events that he hopes will be able to help guide the reader, who at that time were the members of the new *"Spirit filled"* church at Corinth:

6. *Now, brethren, if I come unto you speaking with tongues, what shall I profit you, except I shall speak to you either by revelation, or by knowledge, or by prophesying, or by doctrine?*
7. *And even things without life giving sound, whether pipe or harp, except they give a distinction in the sounds, how shall it be known what is piped or harped?*
8. *For if the trumpet give an uncertain sound, who shall prepare himself to the battle?*
9. *So likewise ye, except ye utter by the tongue words easy to be understood, how shall it be known what is spoken? for ye shall speak into the air.*
10. *There are, it may be, so many kinds of voices in the world, and none of them is without signification.*
11. *Therefore if I know not the meaning of the voice, I shall be unto him that speaketh a barbarian, and he that speaketh shall be a barbarian unto me.*
12. *Even so ye, forasmuch as ye are zealous of spiritual gifts, seek that ye may excel to the edifying of the church.*
13. *Wherefore let him that speaketh in an unknown tongue pray that he may interpret.*
— 1 Corinthians 14: 6–13

When we use these voice gifts in the church we are expected to speak up. Don't shout. Stay calm and speak with a loud and clear voice so all can hear.

If we speak in a soft voice or if we mumble with uncertainty that will not be helpful in a large gathering.

Verses 12 and 13 encourage us again to "*seek*" that we may "*excel to the edifying of the church*" and "*pray*" that we may next use the gift of "*interpretation of tongues.*"

We can ask the Lord to help us step out in faith again, and to give us the words to speak as an interpretation of somebody's message in tongues.

In the next six verses Paul continues to exhort the church at Corinth to do both of these: "*pray with the spirit*" and "*pray with the understanding.*"

> 14. *For if I pray in an unknown tongue, my spirit prayeth, but my understanding is unfruitful.*
> 15. *What is it then? I will pray with the spirit, and I will pray with the understanding also: I will sing with the spirit, and I will sing with the understanding also.*
> 16. *Else when thou shalt bless with the spirit, how shall he that occupieth the room of the unlearned say Amen at thy giving of thanks, seeing he understandeth not what thou sayest?*
> 17. *For thou verily givest thanks well, but the other is not edified.*
> 18. *I thank my God, I speak with tongues more than ye all:*
> 19. *Yet in the church I had rather speak five words with my understanding, that by my voice I might teach others also, than ten thousand words in an unknown tongue.*
> — 1 Corinthians 14: 14–19

Each of these elements has a vital role to play in the church and he reminds us that *"I speak with tongues more than ye all."*

In verse 19 he makes the important point: *"in the church"* he would rather *"speak five words with my understanding"* to help others understand, compared to speaking *"ten thousand words in an unknown tongue."*

Please note — this is *not* one of those at the total exclusion of the other. He could do both of these and expects that the hearers or readers of his letters could also.

He is giving *guidance* in *what we should do* in a public church meeting where we hope there will be *"unlearned"* visitors or onlookers who have not yet, themselves, been *"born again."*

In the next three verses Paul reminds us of the need to be more mature in our understanding:

> 20. *Brethren, be not children in understanding: howbeit in malice be ye children, but in understanding be men.*
> 21. *In the law it is written, With men of other tongues and other lips will I speak unto this people; and yet for all that will they not hear me, saith the Lord.*
> 22. *Wherefore tongues are for a sign, not to them that believe, but to them that believe not: but prophesying serveth not for them that believe not, but for them which believe.*
> — 1 Corinthians 14: 20–22

Verse 22 tells us that *"tongues"* are for a *"sign"* to the unbeliever — so the use of *"tongues"* in a controlled manner is essential in meetings.

Prophesying serves more for listeners whom are themselves born again believers because they have the ability to rightly discern and believe what they hear and this will edify the spirit-filled church.

Paul continues his clear instructions in verse 23, where he tells us to refrain from *"all"* speaking with tongues at once, because any *"unlearned"* visitors would understandably say *"you are mad."*

> 23. *If therefore the whole church be come together into one place, and all speak with tongues, and there come in those that are unlearned, or unbelievers, will they not say that ye are mad?*
> 24. *But if all prophesy, and there come in one that believeth not, or one unlearned, he is convinced of all, he is judged of all:*
> 25. *And thus are the secrets of his heart made manifest; and so falling down on his face he will worship God, and report that God is in you of a truth.*
> 26. *How is it then, brethren? when ye come together, every one of you hath a psalm, hath a doctrine, hath a tongue, hath a revelation, hath an interpretation. Let all things be done unto edifying.*
> — 1 Corinthians 14: 23–26

When we come together, Paul writes: *"Let all things be done unto edifying."*

There's a time and place for tongues. Listen for the pastor to invite their use in the church. Paul describes a little more in the next three verses.

> 27. *If any man speak in an unknown tongue, let it be by two, or at the most by three, and that by course; and let one interpret.*

46

28. *But if there be no interpreter, let him keep silence in the church; and let him speak to himself, and to God.*
29. *Let the prophets speak two or three, and let the other judge.*
— 1 Corinthians 14: 27–29

Important: Two, or *at the most* three, and that by course.

30. *If any thing be revealed to another that sitteth by, let the first hold his peace.*
31. *For ye may all prophesy one by one, that all may learn, and all may be comforted.*
32. *And the spirits of the prophets are subject to the prophets.*
33. *For God is not the author of confusion, but of peace, as in all churches of the saints.*
— 1 Corinthians 14: 30–33

Verse 32 instructs us that we are in full control of the way in which we utilise the gifts of the Spirit. Please use the gifts as described (below) in verse 40: *"decently"* and *"in order."*

Loud talking while a meeting is running is not appreciated. If anything is unclear make a written or mental note and feel free to ask a pastor or other members of the oversight; leaders or elders of the church for the answers to any questions that may get raised in your thinking:

34. *Let your women keep silence in the churches: for it is not permitted unto them to speak; but they are commanded to be under obedience as also saith the law.*
35. *And if they will learn any thing, let them ask their husbands at home: for it is a shame for women to speak in the church.*
— 1 Corinthians 14: 34–35

Laws and expectations may have been somewhat different in Paul's time, although today, we still expect that *all* people will act with some decorum, both women *and* men.

When the meeting is under way we should listen rather than talk to each other at that time. There will be plenty of time for conversation after the meeting concludes.

In the next four verses, 36 to 39, Paul makes the point that we all have access to the Word of God and we should be capable of determining that what he has written to the new church at Corinth is *"the commandments of the Lord:"*

> 36. *What? came the word of God out from you?*
> *or came it unto you only?*
> 37. *If any man think himself to be a prophet, or*
> *spiritual, let him acknowledge that the things that*
> *I write unto you are the commandments of the*
> *Lord.*
> 38. *But if any man be ignorant, let him be*
> *ignorant.*
> 39. *Wherefore, brethren, covet to prophesy, and*
> *forbid not to speak with tongues.*
> — 1 Corinthians 14: 36–39

Paul reminds us once again, that we should *"covet"* (earnestly desire and pray) to use the gift of *"prophecy"* and reminds us that we should *"not forbid"* anyone *"to speak with tongues"* in those ways he has already described for us in great detail.

All three of these voice gifts: *"tongues," "interpretation of tongues"* and *"prophecy"* have their function in the Spirit filled church.

The sentence in the last verse, 40, of 1st Corinthians, chapter 14, admonishes and instructs us to ensure that we always act in a circumspect manner. We need to ensure we do *"all things"* both *"decently and in order:"*

40. *Let all things be done decently and in order.*
— 1 Corinthians 14: 40

The amount of detail in the apostle Paul's writing is extensive. We have, at best, brushed the surface here. It takes time to read what Paul wrote and I expect it will take most of us several attempts to absorb and understand all that he had to say.

Read it in small chunks and re-read those sections that cause any consternation. There is a lot of information to assimilate.

Pray about it. The Spirit of the living God now dwells within us and He will help us understand.

Please speak with your pastors and oversight about any questions you may have. I am sure they will be glad to help.

Chapter 5

Gifts of the Spirit

In addition to gaining the ability to speak in other tongues when we receive the gift of the Holy Spirit, as a result of our *repentance* and *baptism* in water and the grace of Almighty God, we discover there is so much more.

The first eleven verses in 1st Corinthians, chapter 12, expressly discuss the topic of *"spiritual gifts."*

Like the nine *"fruit of the Spirit"* about which we have read in Galatians chapter 5, verses 22 and 23, there's also nine *"spiritual gifts."*

These *"spiritual gifts"* become available for us to use from the moment we get *"born again."*

What are these gifts? What is their purpose? How are they utilised? When is the time for their use? Where do they get used and by whom?

We have read about three of these *"gifts"* in my previous chapter. We already know a considerable amount about the answers to those questions.

The best thing to do, as always, is to read what the Word of God has to say.

Paul begins his discourse on *"spiritual gifts"* with these
words:

> 1. *Now concerning spiritual gifts, brethren, I
> would not have you ignorant.*
> 2. *Ye know that ye were Gentiles, carried away
> unto these dumb idols, even as ye were led.*
> 3. *Wherefore I give you to understand, that no
> man speaking by the Spirit of God calleth Jesus
> accursed: and that no man can say that Jesus is
> the Lord, but by the Holy Ghost.*
> — 1 Corinthians 12:1–3

Paul is writing to the new church at Corinth so they and
this applies to us today, would not be *ignorant* about the
operation of the *"spiritual gifts."*

These gifts get *manifested* by the *"Spirit"* of God. The
"spiritual gifts" are available to all spirit-filled, born-again
people, rightly called Christians — the name means: the
"anointed" ones. See: Acts chapter 11, verse 26.

Even though they would have seen and heard these *"gifts"*
operating in their midst, Paul considers it essential to provide
this guidance.

Verse 3 states that *when* we are *"speaking by the Spirit"*
or *"speaking in other tongues"* we will never call Jesus
"accursed." We will never be speaking any blasphemy
towards God or Jesus or the Holy Spirit.

Even though we do not necessarily understand what we are
saying the Holy Spirit assures us that He will not permit us
to say anything that is in any way wrong.

One might imagine, *if* our thoughts and/or intentions were
less than upright before God, then we may be expressing
those and God may deal with us appropriately.

Rather than *inclining* His ear *toward* us He could turn away and distance Himself from our communication until we sort out our thinking and get back to making a more righteous approach.

Please notice another interesting statement in verse 3. The stipulation of this significant fact: *"no man can say that Jesus is Lord"* (except) *"but by the Holy Ghost."*

This speaks to our new sanctified state with our sins forgiven through the blood of Jesus, ratified by the gift of the *"Holy Ghost"* enabling us truly to call Jesus *"Lord."*

We are unable to *rightly* or *properly* or in a *complete sense* call Jesus *"Lord"* until the time we have received the gift of the Holy Ghost — when we can speak in unlearned tongues.

The writer of Luke reminds us that Jesus said this:

> 46. *And why call ye me, Lord, Lord, and do not the things which I say?*
> — Luke 6:46

Remember, Jesus said we *"must be born again."*

This agrees with what we read in the book of Romans chapter 8, verse 9:

> 9. *But ye are not in the flesh, but in the Spirit, if so be that the Spirit of God dwell in you. Now if any man have not the Spirit of Christ, he is none of his.*
> — Romans 8:9

Receiving the in-filling gift of the Holy Spirit is a mandatory prerequisite — enabling us to say *"Jesus is our Lord."*

In 1st Corinthians chapter 12, verses 4 to 7, Paul discusses the observed differences in the operation and manifestation of these miraculous gifts of the Holy Spirit:

4. *Now there are diversities of gifts, but the same Spirit.*
5. *And there are differences of administrations, but the same Lord.*
6. *And there are diversities of operations, but it is the same God which worketh all in all.*
7. *But the manifestation of the Spirit is given to every man to profit withal.*
— 1 Corinthians 12:4–7

Paul assures us that any perceived differences and diversities of the gifts all emanate from *"the same Spirit,"* *"the same Lord,"* *"the same God."*

He states that each of these is a *"manifestation of the Spirit"* and *"is given to every man to profit withal"* — meaning each of us can use these and they will be of benefit toward our edification and understanding in matters that pertain to our relationship with God.

The next three verses, 8, 9 and 10, of 1st Corinthians, chapter 12, is where Paul specifically names the nine *"spiritual gifts:"*

8. *For to one is given by the Spirit the word of wisdom; to another the word of knowledge by the same Spirit;*
9. *To another faith by the same Spirit; to another the gifts of healing by the same Spirit;*
10. *To another the working of miracles; to another prophecy; to another discerning of spirits; to another divers kinds of tongues; to another the interpretation of tongues:*
— 1 Corinthians 12:8–10

Count them:

1. *word of wisdom,*
2. *word of knowledge,*
3. *faith,*
4. *gifts of healing,*
5. *working of miracles,*
6. *prophecy,*
7. *discerning of spirits,*
8. *divers kinds of tongues,*
9. *interpretation of tongues.*

You may notice that certain people in the church seem to be adept at speaking out with a message in other tongues; at the appointed time.

Others will often speak up and use the gift of interpretation of tongues; in answer to those.

There are people who appear to be comfortable operating the gift of prophecy after those first two gifts get used.

> 11. *But all these worketh that one and the selfsame Spirit, dividing to every man severally as he will.*
> — 1 Corinthians 12:11

Verse 11 says the Spirit divides (or *distributes*) these gifts *"to every man severally as he will."*

Who then can make use of these *"spiritual gifts?"*

Every man and woman who is *"born again"* by the Spirit of God. We get baptised with the gift of the Holy Spirit the same way people experienced on the day of Pentecost when God honoured His promise *"I will pour out of my Spirit upon all flesh."*

We have received the gift of the Holy Spirit with the evidence of speaking in *"other tongues."* Hopefully we have seen our "*faith*" in operation as we pray for "*gifts of healing*" and the "*working of miracles*" for ourselves and others.

The accompanying gifts, manifested as we seek the Lord, will get used as and when we prayerfully request their operation.

Please Note: I realise there is a lot of information contained here. Again I suggest reading it in small parts or digestible chunks and coming back later for more after spending time praying in the precious unlearned tongue that God has given. The Holy Spirit within will assist our understanding.

The prophet Isaiah used these words:

> 10. *For precept must be upon precept, precept upon precept; line upon line, line upon line; here a little, and there a little:*
> — Isaiah 28:10

I don't know about you. I need to absorb new information in small chunks and then move on to the next parts.

Let's take a look at the "*gifts of the Spirit.*"

In the enumerated list below, I have attempted to include a Bible verse or two which may provide a little context for this set of nine miraculous gifts of the Holy Spirit with which The Lord's generosity has provisioned us, the body of the church:

1. **word of wisdom**

> 17. *But the wisdom that is from above is first pure, then peaceable, gentle, and easy to be intreated, full of mercy and good fruits, without partiality, and without hypocrisy.*
> — James 3:17

Words of wisdom from God and His Word get imparted to us by the Holy Spirit. Look at how James describes this "*wisdom from above.*"

As we read the Word of God we can stand in awe at the wisdom contained therein. When we speak to others about the gospel and the kingdom of God we can find ourself saying words we never knew we knew — I know I have. I believe at these times we are expounding the Word of God through the use of this gift; and/or the next *"word of knowledge."*

Look at the opening verses of the first Psalm:

> 1. *Blessed is the man that walketh not in the counsel of the ungodly, nor standeth in the way of sinners, nor sitteth in the seat of the scornful.*
> 2. *But his delight is in the law of the LORD; and in his law doth he meditate day and night.*
> — Psalms 1:1–2

Encouraged to delight ourself in reading God's Word we get astounded by the collective wisdom it contains and by the words that will soon proceed out of our own mouth.

2. word of knowledge

> 6. *For God, who commanded the light to shine out of darkness, hath shined in our hearts, to give the light of the knowledge of the glory of God in the face of Jesus Christ.*
> — 2 Corinthians 4:6

A word or words of knowledge from God and His Word get imparted to us through the inspiration of the Holy Spirit.

The knowledge contained in the Word of God is of utmost importance for us to assimilate. That happens over time.

There are people who can start at Genesis and read all the way through to the book of Revelation. Other people find reading a *"One Year Bible"* where you read a selection of verses from different parts of God's Word each day to be more doable.

Whatever you choose. Read it. Enjoy it. Absorb it.

In the 21st century we can carry a copy of the Bible with us where ever we go using an *"App"* on our smartphone. Learn to use the navigation and search buttons.

Some of these even include audio versions that are easy to listen to while we are on the move. Both reading and listening can help retention.

Remember to give abundant thanks to God for preserving His Word for our ongoing access.

3. faith

Presented to each of us is an everlasting gift *"the measure of faith."* None of us should think we have any more or any less faith than another brother or sister in the Lord:

> 3. *For I say, through the grace given unto me,*
> *to every man that is among you, not to think*
> *of himself more highly than he ought to think;*
> *but to think soberly, according as God hath*
> *dealt to every man the measure of faith.*
> — Romans 12:3

We have all the faith necessary to move mountains, if ever we should have the real *need*:

> 20. *If ye have faith as a grain of mustard*
> *seed, ye shall say unto this mountain, Remove*
> *hence to yonder place; and it shall remove;*
> *and nothing shall be impossible unto you.*
> — Matthew 17:20

Jesus said: *"nothing shall be impossible unto you.*

God's gift of faith gets manifested in us by the Holy Spirit of God.

The *"fruit"* called faith helps us to express our bountiful *"gift"* of faith to others. We can share the gospel with them and encourage them. We can pray for them and expect them to get healed and have their needs met by our gracious God. Always pray believing.

4. gifts of healing

> 35. *And Jesus went about all the cities and villages, teaching in their synagogues, and preaching the gospel of the kingdom, and healing every sickness and every disease among the people.*
> — Matthew 9:35

God's Spirit-filled church has this expectation:

> 14. *Is any sick among you? let him call for the elders of the church; and let them pray over him, anointing him with oil in the name of the Lord:*
> 15. *And the prayer of faith shall save the sick, and the Lord shall raise him up;*
> — James 5:14–15

When we call upon God, He hears and answers our prayers.

As you talk to other people in the church and listen to their testimonies you will discover brothers and sisters who have been miraculously healed from medical problems and diseases like deafness, blindness, speech difficulties, paralysis — even cancer.

5. **working of miracles**

> 3. *How shall we escape, if we neglect so great salvation; which at the first began to be spoken by the Lord, and was confirmed unto us by them that heard him;*
> 4. *God also bearing them witness, both with signs and wonders, and with divers miracles, and gifts of the Holy Ghost, according to his own will?*
> — Hebrews 2:3–4

God provides the *"signs and wonders"* and the diverse *"miracles"* — *"according to his own will."*

The circumstances of life can bring all kinds of difficulties. We pray about these and find that God intervenes on our behalf producing all manner of *"signs and wonders and miracles."*

Do not get concerned if the answer God provides is not as you imagined it should be. We often find as we travel down the road of life that God always knows the end from the beginning and what He provides is far better than whatever we originally had in mind.

Remember to thank God for His ever superior ways.

6. **prophecy**

Consider these verses from 2nd Peter:

> 19. *We have also a more sure word of prophecy; whereunto ye do well that ye take heed, as unto a light that shineth in a dark place, until the day dawn, and the day star arise in your hearts:*
> 20. *Knowing this first, that no prophecy of the scripture is of any private interpretation.*
> 21. *For the prophecy came not in old time by the will of man: but holy men of God spake as they were moved by the Holy Ghost.*

— 2 Peter 1:19–21

Please take note of verse 20 which says *"no prophecy of the scripture is of any private interpretation."*

The prophets who wrote what they did in God's Word got inspired by the Spirit of God. They did not write their own ideas. They got directed by the inspiration of Almighty God.

When we read their words we must not put our own *"spin"* or interpretation on those. Do not take a single phrase or verse out of context. Read the surrounding verses. Do they support your view?

Don't stop there. Read what else the Word of God has to say about the topic and its descriptive words. Always read and cross check with the other scriptures. It's rare, if ever, to find a single verse that stands alone and is nowhere else referenced in God's Word. God in His infinite Wisdom has provided plenty of text to help us see the important truths in His Word.

The words we speak when operating the gift of *"prophecy"* is *not* what *"we think up"* in our own mind. Rather, we speak as we get *"moved by the Holy Ghost."*

Peter also admonishes us to ensure that:

> 11. *If any man speak, let him speak as the oracles of God; if any man minister, let him do it as of the ability which God giveth: that God in all things may be glorified through Jesus Christ, to whom be praise and dominion for ever and ever. Amen.*
> — 1 Peter 4:11

That little word *"Amen"* means we ought to pause and reflect, consider in depth, and contemplate what we have read, or heard.

When we speak, it should always be *"as the oracles of God."*

This means we expect what we hear to *agree* with the Word of God.

We do not expect to hear anything radical and new that is nowhere referenced in God's Word, the Bible.

God does not need our help to write His Word. He has done this for us already. He has spent centuries inspiring and refining the words He wants for our encouragement and learning. Stick to the script.

The Old Testament contains this description of the test for a *"false"* prophet:

> 21. *And if thou say in thine heart, How shall we know the word which the LORD hath not spoken?*
> 22. *When a prophet speaketh in the name of the LORD, if the thing follow not, nor come to pass, that is the thing which the LORD hath not spoken, but the prophet hath spoken it presumptuously: thou shalt not be afraid of him.*
> — Deuteronomy 18:21–22

The same test applies for us today.

We do not want to hear from man's own thoughts and imagination.

We want encouragement by and through *"the oracles of God."*

Our founding Pastor L.R.Longfield used to say: *"The Word of God is more up to date than tomorrow's news."*

Yes. He said *"tomorrow's"* news.

7. discerning of spirits

Consider the words in this verse again:

> 12. *For the word of God is quick, and powerful, and sharper than any twoedged sword, piercing even to the dividing asunder of soul and spirit, and of the joints and marrow, and is a discerner of the thoughts and intents of the heart.*
> — Hebrews 4:12

The Holy Spirit always agrees with the Word of God. He will adequately provide necessary *"discernment."* This is not what *we* think or *we* devise; rather this is what God's Word has already declared.

If ever we hear anybody speaking their own thoughts, and those do not align with the Word of God, this gift, *"discernment of spirits"* could alert us to a discrepancy in what gets said.

Do not be overly anxious. It can happen from time to time. The pastor or leader will probably have a quiet word with them after the meeting.

If ever we have any concerns please speak about those with a pastor or a member of the church oversight.

When we are new in our experience in the Lord it could be our own lack of understanding of what God says in His Word.

Do we under or over estimate the extent of God's promises?

Do not forget to speak with your pastors and with your brothers and sisters in the Lord.

Make a habit of reading and meditating in God's Word.

8. divers kinds of tongues

On the day of Pentecost they observed over fifteen examples of this. See: Acts chapter 2, verses 7 to 11.

The Galilaeans who spoke out in those different languages had *never* learned to speak them before. The gift of *"divers kinds of tongues"* is a miracle from God, through the operation of the Holy Spirit.

Paul was ever ready to express his commitment to praying in other, unknown, unlearned tongues:

> 18. *I thank my God, I speak with tongues more than ye all:*
> — 1 Corinthians 14:18

Our own *"unlearned tongue"* could begin to sound the same one day. We could wonder: "Did I make this up?" Do not let this concern you. We can put our faith into action and ask God to activate *this* precious gift in our life. We should be in line for a wonderful surprise.

9. interpretation of tongues

For clarity, it bears reading these verses again. They provide the context for using this gift in the church:

> 26. *How is it then, brethren? when ye come together, every one of you hath a psalm, hath a doctrine, hath a tongue, hath a revelation, hath an interpretation. Let all things be done unto edifying.*
> 27. *If any man speak in an unknown tongue, let it be by two, or at the most by three, and that by course; and let one interpret.*
> 28. *But if there be no interpreter, let him keep silence in the church; and let him speak to himself, and to God.*
> — 1 Corinthians 14:26–28

In a church meeting, when invited by the pastor, we operate those voice gifts of the Holy Spirit:

"tongues," "interpretation of tongues" and *"prophecy."*

If we have not yet operated one or more of these three gifts, we can pray to God to ask His blessing on our request to get used in this way.

In the church I attend, there is a brief opportunity for the operation of two or at the most three, messages in *tongues*; with each of those followed by an *interpretation of tongues* and then a time for two or at the most three gifts of *prophecy.*

In a small meeting there could be no one who has operated the gift of *"interpretation of tongues."*

If the pastor or leader knows this and if there are visitors in the meeting, the apostle Paul recommended we should *"keep silence in the church"* — meaning we do not speak out in other tongues.

The pastor or leader could shorten the normal time allotted to the operation of the spiritual gifts for a reason such as that.

God asks us to do everything *"decently and in order."*

The gracious *"promise of the Father"* provides the prayer language with which we can communicate directly to God.

This wonderful *"gift of the Holy Ghost"* also provides other special and identifiable features that Paul called the *"fruit"* and *"gifts"* of the Spirit.

Over time we can learn about these and begin to appreciate them as they come to operate in different ways in our life.

The following verse reminds us to maintain a strong sense of *"charity"* from the Greek word *"agape"* which is *"the love of God"* as we operate:

> 2. *And though I have the gift of prophecy, and understand all mysteries, and all knowledge; and though I have all faith, so that I could remove mountains, and have not charity, I am nothing.*
> — 1 Corinthians 13:2

Our life in the knowledge and understanding of the kingdom of God begins to take shape. Making the first steps with a new found *"fear"* or great *"respect"* for God and His Son Jesus Christ surely marks a true *"beginning of wisdom."* The Psalmist wrote these beautiful words for us:

> 10. *The fear of the LORD is the beginning of wisdom: a good understanding have all they that do his commandments: his praise endureth for ever.*
> — Psalm 111:10

The more we apply ourselves to comprehending what we read and hear from our pastots we find *"the eyes of our understanding get enlightened."*

> 17. *That the God of our Lord Jesus Christ, the Father of glory, may give unto you the spirit of wisdom and revelation in the knowledge of him:*
> 18. *The eyes of your understanding being enlightened; that ye may know what is the hope of his calling, and what the riches of the glory of his inheritance in the saints,*
> — Ephesians 1:17–18

Consider these precious and beautiful and enriching words we read as Paul expounds further upon what he finds *"God has revealed"* unto us *"by his Spirit."* Soak in each remarkable verse:

9. *But as it is written, Eye hath not seen, nor ear heard, neither have entered into the heart of man, the things which God hath prepared for them that love him.*

10. *But God hath revealed them unto us by his Spirit: for the Spirit searcheth all things, yea, the deep things of God.*

11. *For what man knoweth the things of a man, save the spirit of man which is in him? even so the things of God knoweth no man, but the Spirit of God.*

12. *Now we have received, not the spirit of the world, but the spirit which is of God; that we might know the things that are freely given to us of God.*

13. *Which things also we speak, not in the words which man's wisdom teacheth, but which the Holy Ghost teacheth; comparing spiritual things with spiritual.*

14. *But the natural man receiveth not the things of the Spirit of God: for they are foolishness unto him: neither can he know them, because they are spiritually discerned.*

— 1 Corinthians 2:9–14

Verse 14 tells us that in our *"natural"* state before we get *"born again"* we are incapable of understanding *"the things of the Spirit of God"* because they are as *"foolishness"* to us.

They make no sense to the natural man.

These matters get properly *"discerned"* by those who have received the miraculous in-filling of the precious gift of the Holy Ghost through the gracious *"promise of the Father."*

Jesus told Nicodemus that *"Except a man be born again, he cannot see the kingdom of God"* and *"Except a man be born of water and of the Spirit, he cannot enter into the kingdom of God."*

As I started to read the Bible *after* I got born again I found that words and phrases in God's Word began to make sense. The words almost leapt off the page and into my comprehension. No longer were they foolishness to me.

Under my own steam — before I got born again — I had managed to read one or two chapters from Genesis and then in Matthew. I might have managed a Psalm or two. Not much more.

After receiving God's gift of the Holy Spirit I found I wanted to examine more from God's Word because I was understanding what I read. The Bible was talking about me. God's Word is talking to us!

The middle section of writing in 1st Corinthians, chapter 12, in verses 12 to 27, uses the analogy of the members of our bodies (hands, eyes, ears, etc.) to describe how we are to consider ourselves as essential members of the body of Christ. The first three of those verses read:

> 12. *For as the body is one, and hath many members, and all the members of that one body, being many, are one body: so also is Christ.*
> 13. *For by one Spirit are we all baptized into one body, whether we be Jews or Gentiles, whether we be bond or free; and have been all made to drink into one Spirit.*
> 14. *For the body is not one member, but many.*
> — 1 Corinthians 12:12–14

We come from different walks of life. At our churches here in Australia we have come from different countries and cultures. We range in age from children to teenagers and young adults through to middle aged and those more mature in years. We have different levels of confidence and ability to interact with others.

Paul reminds us that each member in a human body has its own unique purpose. Feet do what feet do, hands do what hands do, an eye does what the eye does and so on. Every one of those individual members of a body is vital to enable the body to operate and function as it should.

In the same sense we observe different component parts, different functioning and different capabilities within the members of the church. Now collectively called *"the body of Christ."*

We must consider each of our brothers and sisters in the church as vital, necessary, equal and valuable members of the body of Christ that God has set according to His pleasure:

> 18. *But now hath God set the members every one of them in the body, as it hath pleased him.*
> — 1 Corinthians 12:18

In verse 25, Paul instructs us that we must not ignore or exclude people or permit any schism (*division*) within the church and that we should have the same care one for another. Make your brothers and sisters feel welcome.

We all depend on the functioning of others to operate as the whole representation of the kingdom or realm of God that He intends.

The verses 28 to 31, in the rest of 1st Corinthians, chapter 12, discuss some elements of the distribution of the Spiritual gifts.

They are somewhat different and we may not all be in the practise of exercising *every* gift, although we certainly can when we need and if we will pray to do so.

Paul encourages us to *"covet earnestly the best gifts,"* those that *"edify"* the church and to consider *"a more excellent way:"*

28. *And God hath set some in the church, first apostles, secondarily prophets, thirdly teachers, after that miracles, then gifts of healings, helps, governments, diversities of tongues.*
29. *Are all apostles? are all prophets? are all teachers? are all workers of miracles?*
30. *Have all the gifts of healing? do all speak with tongues? do all interpret?*
31. *But covet earnestly the best gifts: and yet shew I unto you a more excellent way.*
— 1 Corinthians 12:28–31

In summary — the heavenly Father, Who is Omniscient — All Knowing in His wisdom, has equipped us with this set of wonderful, personal and miraculous gifts of the Holy Spirit:

1. *word of wisdom,*
2. *word of knowledge,*
3. *faith,*
4. *gifts of healing,*
5. *working of miracles,*
6. *prophecy,*
7. *discerning of spirits,*
8. *divers kinds of tongues,*
9. *interpretation of tongues.*

God's Word encourages us to make use of these gifts. Some of them require a little bit of effort and the boldness to trust God and to open our mouth at the appropriate time.

Some of us may be shy, or self-conscious and it can be easier to make a start with the gifts of *"tongues"* and then *"interpretation"* and next a *"prophecy"* in the smaller meetings of the church.

There are no hard and fast rules about the order in which we start. We could first get moved to utter words of interpretation for a message in other tongues. Keep it short and sharp and to the point. God knows our power of concentration is limited.

Get led by the Spirit of the Living God that now dwells inside and take guidance from the requests of the pastor or leader of the meeting.

The first time is the hardest. It will encourage other members of the church to hear us speak out. We will soon get over any "*nerves*" we may experience.

We will have *already* spoken in "*tongues*" and if we have not already done so we can ask God to enable "*diversity*" in our tongue. We trust and believe there will soon be a pleasant surprise.

Remember, God is there with us. He dwells *inside* us by His Spirit, to help, to guide and to provide us with the words to say.

We should not try to make up the words by ourselves — rather, we ask, pray and wait for the words of God to come flowing so these can roll off the tongue without needing to think.

We want to hear Words from Almighty God *not* words from our own imagination. This will happen, miraculously if we will ask Him believing.

We need to be reading the Word of God to help this process because everything we say will be, *not always* the reciting of a Bible text, word for word, but *rather,* words provided through the Spirit and these will be *in agreement with what God is already saying* in His Word.

Paul discusses the "*more excellent way*" in 1st Corinthians, chapter 13, where he *emphasises* the need for us to ensure that whatever we do we must do that with "*charity*" utilising the first-mentioned "*fruit*" of the Spirit: "*love*" which is "*agape*" the "*love of God:*"

He commences with these words:

> 1. *Though I speak with the tongues of men and of angels, and have not charity, I am become as sounding brass, or a tinkling cymbal.*
> 2. *And though I have the gift of prophecy, and understand all mysteries, and all knowledge; and though I have all faith, so that I could remove mountains, and have not charity, I am nothing.*
> 3. *And though I bestow all my goods to feed the poor, and though I give my body to be burned, and have not charity, it profiteth me nothing.*
> — 1 Corinthians 13:1–3

We must use these "*gifts of the Spirit*" with wisdom and with "*charity.*"

They do not constitute a set of toys that we can splash around and leave scattered all over the floor like an immature child.

Miraculous gifts provided through the in-filling of the Holy Ghost in us. Intended for use within the members of the church, the body of Christ.

Paul provides the following exposition on the true meaning of "*charity:*"

> 4. *Charity suffereth long, and is kind; charity envieth not; charity vaunteth not itself, is not puffed up,*
> 5. *Doth not behave itself unseemly, seeketh not her own, is not easily provoked, thinketh no evil;*
> 6. *Rejoiceth not in iniquity, but rejoiceth in the truth;*

*7. Beareth all things, believeth all things, hopeth
all things, endureth all things.*
— 1 Corinthians 13:4–7

The *"agape"* love of God is vastly superior to the love natural
man exhibits. Read those verses again and consider how far
short we fall.

Remember how Peter the apostle stood up on the day of
Pentecost and instructed the gathering crowd:

> 38. *Then Peter said unto them, Repent, and be
> baptized every one of you in the name of Jesus
> Christ for the remission of sins, and ye shall
> receive the gift of the Holy Ghost.*
> — Acts 2:38

I have often wondered if Peter, on that day, had any real
understanding of the importance of the provision of God's
wonderful gift?

He received this gift himself earlier the same day. I expect
he knew more than that for which I give him credit. He had
walked and talked with Jesus.

He and others of those 120 people were certainly manifesting
gifts of the Spirit which included: *"word of wisdom," "word
of knowledge," "faith,"* and they all heard examples of *"divers
kinds of tongues,"* because in Acts, chapter 2, we can read:

> 4. *And they were all filled with the Holy Ghost,
> and began to speak with other tongues, as the
> Spirit gave them utterance.*
> 5. *And there were dwelling at Jerusalem Jews,
> devout men, out of every nation under heaven.*
> 6. *Now when this was noised abroad, the multitude
> came together, and were confounded, because that
> every man heard them speak in his own language.*

7. And they were all amazed and marvelled,
saying one to another, Behold, are not all these
which speak Galilaeans?
8. And how hear we every man in our own
tongue, wherein we were born?
9. Parthians, and Medes, and Elamites, and the
dwellers in Mesopotamia, and in Judaea, and
Cappadocia, in Pontus, and Asia,
10. Phrygia, and Pamphylia, in Egypt, and in
the parts of Libya about Cyrene, and strangers
of Rome, Jews and proselytes,
11. Cretes and Arabians, we do hear them speak
in our tongues the wonderful works of God.
— Acts 2:4–11

Earlier, I made a point that speaking in tongues is the method by which we pray directly to God; and this is true.

In verses 6 and 8 of the above passage from Acts 2, we see that at special times these other *"unlearned tongues"* is miraculously capable of being the *foreign* languages that other people fluently speak. Look at that long list of languages in verses 9 to 11.

We need to understand *"they were all amazed"* because those who spoke *"the wonderful works of God"* in those foreign tongues had *never* before learned to speak those languages.

Read verse 7 again. They were *"Galilaeans,"* people who in those days were not expected to travel in wide enough circles to enable them to speak one or two foreign languages, let alone fifteen.

That is the miracle of those diverse other tongues the crowd of onlookers heard on that day of Pentecost.

In general, our personal *"unlearned tongues"* is the manner by which we make our direct communications, that is, our individual worship and prayer to God. This is through the agency of the Holy Spirit that the Creator has graciously delivered to each of us.

In 1st Corinthians, chapter 13, verse 1, you could have noticed that Paul mentions the term *"tongues of men and of angels."*

At most times we may never understand precisely what we are saying. We can rejoice because God will always know.

Look at these beautiful words in Romans chapter 8:

> 26. *Likewise the Spirit also helpeth our infirmities: for we know not what we should pray for as we ought: but the Spirit itself maketh intercession for us with groanings which cannot be uttered.*
> — Romans 8:26

How good is that? The Holy Spirit inside us now helps us to say the words we need to say to God to express our innermost thoughts and feelings.

When we pray in other tongues our communication is direct to God on a one to One basis. We can pour out our heart and soul. We can rejoice in all that He provides and for the way He cares. We can give God all the glory for His wonderful plan of salvation.

We can praise and thank Jesus Christ for all He went through and for the victory He gained over death. We have a hope that one day we will get caught up to live forever with Him and with the heavenly Father.

We should know and believe that praying in other tongues is good for us.

Why? Because verse 20, in the small book of Jude informs us that *"praying in the Holy Ghost,"* which we now know is *"praying in tongues,"* has the action of *"building up yourselves."*

> 20. *But ye, beloved, building up yourselves on*
> *your most holy faith, praying in the Holy Ghost,*
> 21. *Keep yourselves in the love of God, looking for*
> *the mercy of our Lord Jesus Christ unto eternal*
> *life.*
> — Jude 1:20–21

Please note that Jude does *not* say that *"praying in the Holy Ghost"* will *"increase"* or *"build up"* our *"faith."*

He says *"praying in the Holy Ghost"* will help in *"building up yourselves"* on or through the use of *"your most holy faith."*

Why? Because faith is a *"fruit"* or expression of the Spirit. See: Galatians chapter 5, verse 22.

Now we know that faith is also a *"gift"* of the Spirit. See: 1 Corinthians chapter 12, verse 9.

We also read that God's Word declares we *all* get *"dealt the measure of faith."* We get given the perfect amount of faith. See: Romans chapter 12, verse 3.

We ourselves need the building up and *"praying in the Holy Ghost"* will admirably achieve that task for us.

In my previous chapter we read that Paul instructed that we *"forbid not to speak with tongues."* He also informed us that: *"I speak with tongues more than ye all."*

No doubt this is an important part of the reason that Paul became a most effective minister of the gospel. Historians estimate he travelled more than 10,000 kilometres (over 6,400 miles) during his three recorded missionary journeys across the region; in a time span of about 9 years.

Essentially, we should understand that God has given us all the faith that we will ever need. We should be certain to make good use of it. We have the same *"measure of faith"* as do each of our brothers and sisters in the Lord. They do not get any more. We do not get any less.

God, who is here named *"the Father of Lights,"* is the giver of every good and perfect gift:

> 17. *Every good gift and every perfect gift is from above, and cometh down from the Father of lights, with whom is no variableness, neither shadow of turning.*
> — James 1:17

The promise of the Father delivers to each of us *"good"* and *"perfect"* gifts. Rejoice in the knowledge of His infinite wisdom.

Chapter 6

Walk by faith

When we get *"born again,"* we have a totally new lease on life. If you are an 80 year old you may *not* instantly have the energy of an 18 year old.

What I mean is — we will begin to see life from a new perspective, through the inspiration of God.

No longer are we entirely constrained by our own abilities, whether physical, mental or other capabilities, or the lack thereof.

We now know we have the gift of faith — even the perfect measure of faith in us and this means we can deal with anything that comes our way — through our prayer to God.

If we have not yet done so, the Word of God recommends that from this day forward, we determine in our heart and mind, to perform what is right.

What did Jesus say?

> 16. *And, behold, one came and said unto him, Good Master, what good thing shall I do, that I may have eternal life?*
> 17. *And he said unto him, Why callest thou*

me good? there is none good but one, that is,
God: but if thou wilt enter into life, keep the
commandments.
18. *He saith unto him, Which? Jesus said, Thou*
shalt do no murder, Thou shalt not commit
adultery, Thou shalt not steal, Thou shalt not bear
false witness,
19. *Honour thy father and thy mother: and, Thou*
shalt love thy neighbour as thyself.
20. *The young man saith unto him, All these*
things have I kept from my youth up: what lack
I yet?
21. *Jesus said unto him, If thou wilt be perfect, go*
and sell that thou hast, and give to the poor, and
thou shalt have treasure in heaven: and come and
follow me.
— Matthew 19:16–21

The instruction Jesus gave is unambiguous.

Jesus says we must keep God's commandments and God says
we must do what Jesus commands. Remember God says:
"Hear ye Him."

Life today is complex. That is no excuse. If ever there's
any doubt, as concerns what is right or wrong, please ask
a member of your church oversight, a pastor, an elder or a
house-leader.

Filled with the gift of the Holy Spirit, we know better now.
Yes, we may stumble, on occasion and need to pick up
ourselves from our faults. We need to spend time praying
about our own shortcomings and ask God to help us make
amends, if needs be.

He is a forgiving God, but we need to be honest with Him,
prepared to make the effort to change for the better. We
have no right to break God's laws and commandments
and instructions and guidelines. He has made these for His

purpose and I am sure we do not yet understand the full extent of that.

God knows our *thoughts:*

> 11. *The LORD knoweth the thoughts of man, that they are vanity.*
> — Psalms 94:11

We can hide nothing from Him. When you think about it, this is *always* the best basis, for an open and meaningful relationship with anybody, and in particular, with God.

We can still get ourselves into a muddle at times, and think that God is going to supply everything we zealously think we *want*, rather than what He has promised, that is, our *needs:*

> 19. *But my God shall supply all your need according to his riches in glory by Christ Jesus.*
> — Philippians 4:19

I hope it could help to read examples showing how Jesus and His disciples went about healing the sick.

Consider this example when Jesus prayed for ten lepers:

> 11. *And it came to pass, as he went to Jerusalem, that he passed through the midst of Samaria and Galilee.*
> 12. *And as he entered into a certain village, there met him ten men that were lepers, which stood afar off:*
> 13. *And they lifted up their voices, and said, Jesus, Master, have mercy on us.*
> 14. *And when he saw them, he said unto them, Go shew yourselves unto the priests. And it came to pass, that, as they went, they were cleansed.*

15. *And one of them, when he saw that he was healed, turned back, and with a loud voice glorified God,*

16. *And fell down on his face at his feet, giving him thanks: and he was a Samaritan.*

17. *And Jesus answering said, Were there not ten cleansed? but where are the nine?*

18. *There are not found that returned to give glory to God, save this stranger.*

19. *And he said unto him, Arise, go thy way: thy faith hath made thee whole.*

— Luke 17:11–19

Verse 14 says that *"as they went, they were cleansed."* One of the ten turned around and gave thanks and glorified God. In verse 19 Jesus says *"thy faith hath made thee whole."*

The gospel of Matthew tells us that Jesus gave His disciples *"power to heal all manner of sickness and disease:"*

1. *And when he had called unto him his twelve disciples, he gave them power against unclean spirits, to cast them out, and to heal all manner of sickness and all manner of disease.*

— Matthew 10:1

Here is an example where the disciples of Jesus were unable to heal the *"sore vexed"* son of a man who had sought help from them:

14. *And when they were come to the multitude, there came to him a certain man, kneeling down to him, and saying,*

15. *Lord, have mercy on my son: for he is lunatick, and sore vexed: for ofttimes he falleth into the fire, and oft into the water.*

16. *And I brought him to thy disciples, and they could not cure him.*
17. *Then Jesus answered and said, O faithless and perverse generation, how long shall I be with you? how long shall I suffer you? bring him hither to me.*
18. *And Jesus rebuked the devil; and he departed out of him: and the child was cured from that very hour.*
— Matthew 17:14–18

The disciples asked Jesus why they had failed:

19. *Then came the disciples to Jesus apart, and said, Why could not we cast him out?*
20. *And Jesus said unto them, Because of your unbelief: for verily I say unto you, If ye have faith as a grain of mustard seed, ye shall say unto this mountain, Remove hence to yonder place; and it shall remove; and nothing shall be impossible unto you.*
21. *Howbeit this kind goeth not out but by prayer and fasting.*
— Matthew 17:19–21

Jesus said: *"Because of your unbelief."* Jesus encouraged them and now encourages us by saying: *"If ye have faith as a grain of mustard seed,"* then *"nothing shall be impossible unto you."*

We are not expected to go about moving an enormous physical mountain out of it's appointed location every day. Think of *"mountain"* as meaning: *"hard, difficult or humanly impossible"* situations.

Please note — Jesus did not expect the person suffering such an illness or trauma to be the one who must *"pray and fast."*

That is a responsibility for us, the healthy, *"born again,"* believing members of the church to do. If *"we"* will believe then no doubt, soon the one with the *"infirmity"* will recover. If not, then *"we"* could need to pray and fast more. Not them!

By the way, if we pray for healing from an otherwise incurable disease, and it does not disappear in an instant, we do *not* stop using whatever help the medical world can provide, to spite our face!

We never tell people with any infirmity to diminish or stop taking their prescribed medicines or treatment.

God is well able to do what He does, despite what we may need to help us stay alive and/or help us live in a more comfortable manner.

We have read about the difficulties the disciples of Jesus had. Not everything is plain sailing and will happen at the drop of a hat! Yet Jesus reminded His disciples they needed no more than: *"faith"* as a small *"grain of mustard seed!"*

Remember that *"faith"* is a gift from God. We do not even need to find our own speck of faith.

Here is a marvelous story of how Jesus healed a young 12 year old girl. Her father had received the news to say *"Thy daughter is dead"*:

> 35. *While he yet spake, there came from the ruler of the synagogue's house certain which said, Thy daughter is dead: why troublest thou the Master any further?*
> 36. *As soon as Jesus heard the word that was spoken, he saith unto the ruler of the synagogue, Be not afraid, only believe.*
> 37. *And he suffered no man to follow him, save Peter, and James, and John the brother of James.*
> 38. *And he cometh to the house of the ruler of the*

*synagogue, and seeth the tumult, and them that
wept and wailed greatly.
39. And when he was come in, he saith unto
them, Why make ye this ado, and weep? the
damsel is not dead, but sleepeth.
40. And they laughed him to scorn. But when he
had put them all out, he taketh the father and the
mother of the damsel, and them that were with
him, and entereth in where the damsel was lying.
41. And he took the damsel by the hand, and
said unto her, Talitha cumi; which is, being
interpreted, Damsel, I say unto thee, arise.
42. And straightway the damsel arose, and walked;
for she was of the age of twelve years. And they
were astonished with a great astonishment.
43. And he charged them straitly that no man
should know it; and commanded that something
should be given her to eat.*
— Mark 5:35–43

Look at what Jesus said in verse 36: *"Be not afraid, only
believe."*

In verse 40 we see that people laughed at Jesus. No matter,
He *"put them all out,"* except the father and the mother and
His disciples and then exercised His faith in His heavenly
Father, God.

There's no need for any underhanded theatrics.

In the book of James, we find this sage advice:

*6. But let him ask in faith, nothing wavering. For
he that wavereth is like a wave of the sea driven
with the wind and tossed.
7. For let not that man think that he shall receive
any thing of the Lord.*

8. *A double minded man is unstable in all his ways.*
— James 1:6–8

Before we got Spirit Filled we could have been prone to hopping from one foot to the other, always uncertain about which way to go.

The Word of God reminds us that we need to exercise certainty when we make our requests to God using the perfect gift of faith He has given us.

We get born again by the power of God. He is all powerful. He will never fail us when we ask with a simple, child-like, unwavering faith in Him.

Here is another story where Jesus heals a leper:

40. *And there came a leper to him, beseeching him, and kneeling down to him, and saying unto him, If thou wilt, thou canst make me clean.*
41. *And Jesus, moved with compassion, put forth his hand, and touched him, and saith unto him, I will; be thou clean.*
42. *And as soon as he had spoken, immediately the leprosy departed from him, and he was cleansed.*
— Mark 1:40–42

We need to understand it's God's will to heal us. It's God's will to provide our every need.

He may not give us three square meals of fish and potatoes every day for the rest of our lives. He could well introduce us to somebody who can help us learn how to go fishing and catch fish or how to cultivate the soil and produce our own food.

Consider these words of advice from Paul to the church at Thessalonica:

> 10. *For even when we were with you, this we commanded you, that if any would not work, neither should he eat.*
> 11. *For we hear that there are some which walk among you disorderly, working not at all, but are busybodies.*
> 12. *Now them that are such we command and exhort by our Lord Jesus Christ, that with quietness they work, and eat their own bread.*
> — 2 Thessalonians 3:10–12

None of us should want to be a burden on society. In general it's expected we will *"work and eat our own bread."*

Don't limit God by saying *"I can't work"* or *"I can't learn."* Prepare yourself for a miracle and say *"I'll try"* and *"I'll give it a go."*

Of course there can be exceptions. Do not let that stop us from calling on God. He promises He will answer if we will call.

I find it helpful to remind myself about God's credentials. He is the Creator of all we can observe. He is all powerful, He knows all there is to know, He is every where and is listening for our call.

We need do nothing other than ask believing. We do not put our own conditions on the way God can answer. God knows far more than we understand. Always remember to give Him the thanks for everything.

There's no need for any uncertainty.

We put our faith into action *before* we pray, and *believe* that God hears and answers our prayers.

In another case Mark reports:

> 23. *Jesus said unto him, If thou canst believe, all*
> *things are possible to him that believeth.*
> — Mark 9:23

And elsewhere:

> 27. *And Jesus looking upon them saith, With men*
> *it is impossible, but not with God: for with God all*
> *things are possible.*
> — Mark 10:27

Like Jesus we do not make a big song and dance about it.
It's not us who does the saving or the healing or who makes
the provision for our need. God is the source of all those
miracles. Remember to give sincere thanks to Him on a
continual basis.

Soon after the day of Pentecost as described starting from
the third chapter of Acts, we can read that the *"born again"*
disciples and other believers found that they could call on the
power of God to heal people through their faith and prayers:

> 1. *Now Peter and John went up together into the*
> *temple at the hour of prayer, being the ninth hour.*
> 2. *And a certain man lame from his mother's*
> *womb was carried, whom they laid daily at the*
> *gate of the temple which is called Beautiful, to ask*
> *alms of them that entered into the temple;*
> 3. *Who seeing Peter and John about to go into*
> *the temple asked an alms.*
> 4. *And Peter, fastening his eyes upon him with*
> *John, said, Look on us.*
> 5. *And he gave heed unto them, expecting to*
> *receive something of them.*

6. *Then Peter said, Silver and gold have I none;*
but such as I have give I thee: In the name of
Jesus Christ of Nazareth rise up and walk.
7. *And he took him by the right hand, and lifted*
him up: and immediately his feet and ankle bones
received strength.
8. *And he leaping up stood, and walked, and*
entered with them into the temple, walking, and
leaping, and praising God.
— Acts 3:1–8

Peter's faith to say *"In the name of Jesus Christ of Nazareth*
rise up and walk" resulted in this man who was lame from
birth getting healed by God and he *"went with them into the*
temple, walking, and leaping, and praising God."

Of course the disciples also wanted to be about the Lord's
business and were keen to preach the gospel to everyone they
could reach:

1. *And as they spake unto the people, the priests,*
and the captain of the temple, and the Sadducees,
came upon them,
2. *Being grieved that they taught the people, and*
preached through Jesus the resurrection from the
dead.
3. *And they laid hands on them, and put them in*
hold unto the next day: for it was now eventide.
4. *Howbeit many of them which heard the word*
believed; and the number of the men was about five
thousand.
— Acts 4:1–4

The disciples and believers needed to cope with difficult
times. Often they were sorely mistreated. A lot of people did
not want to defer to God's authority, even though they could
see and hear about the ongoing miracles.

Look at verse 4 to see the gracious result of their faithful preaching. How wonderful. Another 5,000 people believed.

That makes a total of over 8,120 people before we have read through one seventh of the 28 chapters contained in the book of Acts.

From the moment God honoured His promise to pour out of His Spirit upon all flesh this miracle re-birth became available to us — to everyone, everywhere.

Not everyone wants to hear the good news today. That is their choice. We feel sad for them and pray that one day they may have a change of heart.

Events throughout life can help people to change. God and Jesus could have other, express ideas. Consider Saul of Tarsus, who got apprehended by *"a light from heaven"* while he was travelling on the road to Damascus. We can read about that in Acts chapter 9, verses 1 to 31. Later Saul changed his name to Paul and became the great missionary who spread God's Word far and wide.

Other New Testament books: Romans, Corinthians, Galatians, Ephesians, Philippians, and the like, contain descriptions of information that became clear after those initial events recorded in the book of Acts that we have spent some time reading. Not that we have covered all those!

It turns out that Paul wrote twelve or thirteen of the books we find there. The remaining books got written by authors like Peter, and James, and John, and Jude. They were all *"born again"* by the power of God's gracious *"promise of the Father."*

Consider these two verses:

> 10. *And if Christ be in you, the body is dead because of sin; but the Spirit is life because of righteousness.*

11. *But if the Spirit of him that raised up Jesus
from the dead dwell in you, he that raised up
Christ from the dead shall also quicken your
mortal bodies by his Spirit that dwelleth in you.*
— Romans 8:10–11

That is us now! *"The Spirit of him"* (Almighty God) *"that
raised up Jesus from the dead"* now dwells in those who get
"born again."

If you can believe it, and we certainly should: we are now by
the Holy Spirit made *like* Jesus.

Jesus got born with a mortal body. Everything changed in a
most dramatic way when He got baptized in water by John
the Baptist and the Holy Spirit descended upon Him.

Everything changes for us when we receive what Jesus called
"the promise of the Father" and we get baptized with the
Holy Spirit like He did.

We walk forward in our new found faith. Our faith is now
a *"gift"* given in perfect measure from the Holy Spirit and
we can express the characteristics of our faith through the
"fruit" that the Spirit brings.

We call upon God for His help. We pray for healing and
expect to get healed. We pray for miracles and expect God to
supply our every need. We ask in faith. We do not demand.

We make our petition to God and outline what we think we
need. Next we rejoice in what God provides because we know
that He knows precisely what we need.

We rejoice with the body of Christ and give abundant praises
to God and to Jesus and to the Holy Spirit.

Those three identities represent the eternal power and might
of Almighty God, the grace and mercy of His Son Jesus
Christ and their ability to dwell within us by the Holy Spirit
— the Comforter — the promise of the Father.

Knowing God on a personal basis is a wonderful and glorious experience — a friendship we never expect we can ever hope to make.

We can talk with God at any time of the day or night and know that He hears and responds to everything we say. Never forget to pray to God using the precious unlearned tongue He has given to us.

Praying in other tongues helps us to say what we need to say and also helps us to say what God wants to hear from us.

There's no secrets between us. We are always an open book before His discerning eyes. Now God has given us of His own Spirit to enable us to read and understand the open pages of His Word.

We can now learn about His will and His purpose and His plans for the eternal future He has allowed us to enter. Rejoice in God's grace as we walk on in His gift of faith.

Chapter 7

Preaching the gospel

In answer to the age old question: "*What is the meaning of life?*" a brother in the Lord once responded: "*Life is a time where you have the opportunity to decide if you want to be a part of the Family of God — for eternity.*"

Part of our responsibility to God now that He has graciously filled us with His Holy Spirit is to share the good news with other people. Family and friends, acquaintances, complete strangers, the whomsoever.

Jesus gave us this vital instruction:

> 15. *And he said unto them, Go ye into all the world, and preach the gospel to every creature.*
> — Mark 16:15

In the book of Romans we are reminded of the necessity to exercise our part in spreading the gospel, with these words:

> 14. *How then shall they call on him in whom they have not believed? and how shall they believe in him of whom they have not heard? and how shall they hear without a preacher?*

— Romans 10:14

If we do not speak, then who will?

The outpouring of God's Spirit upon all flesh through what Jesus called: *"the promise of the Father"* is the most precious information the world affords — all because Jesus Christ chose to be obedient to God's will:

> 39. *And he came out, and went, as he was wont, to the mount of Olives; and his disciples also followed him.*
> 40. *And when he was at the place, he said unto them, Pray that ye enter not into temptation.*
> 41. *And he was withdrawn from them about a stone's cast, and kneeled down, and prayed,*
> 42. *Saying, Father, if thou be willing, remove this cup from me: nevertheless not my will, but thine, be done.*
> 43. *And there appeared an angel unto him from heaven, strengthening him.*
> 44. *And being in an agony he prayed more earnestly: and his sweat was as it were great drops of blood falling down to the ground.*
> — Luke 22:39–44

It is difficult for us to understand the perfection of God and the reasons why God's own Son, Jesus Christ, needed to die in our place. I expect we will find out one day — when we see Him face to face.

We give great praise and thanks to Jesus Christ for enduring such torment and we give praises to God for enabling Him to carry that through.

Initially the outpouring of God's Spirit on all flesh began to take place on the day of Pentecost almost 2,000 years ago.

Peter stood up to speak to a gathering crowd and in answer to the question they asked: *"What shall we do?"* he gave everyone these clear instructions:

> 38. *Then Peter said unto them, Repent, and be baptized every one of you in the name of Jesus Christ for the remission of sins, and ye shall receive the gift of the Holy Ghost.*
> 39. *For the promise is unto you, and to your children, and to all that are afar off, even as many as the LORD our God shall call.*
> — Acts 2:38–39

We have already read how thousands of people responded to those words, and found the exact result as Peter described. No doubt, thrilled with their new experience.

Soon, Peter got called, convinced by a vision from God, to preach the gospel to a man from *another* nation: Cornelius, a Roman Centurion, and to his household with a gathering of his *"kinsmen and near friends."*

Even though the Word of God has described the coming of this wonderful and universal event for centuries, their contemporary religious experts did not fully understand what they had read in their own ancient scrolls.

Those in Jerusalem were *astonished* when Peter explained the result of his preaching:

> 15. *And as I began to speak, the Holy Ghost fell on them, as on us at the beginning.*
> — Acts 11:15

He continued to describe:

> 16. *Then remembered I the word of the Lord, how that he said, John indeed baptized with water; but ye shall be baptized with the Holy Ghost.*

17. *Forasmuch then as God gave them the like gift as he did unto us, who believed on the Lord Jesus Christ; what was I, that I could withstand God?*
— Acts 11:16–17

Those already *"born again"* people in Jerusalem, from the house of Israel came to realise:

18. *When they heard these things, they held their peace, and glorified God, saying, Then hath God also to the Gentiles granted repentance unto life.*
— Acts 11:18

Together we rejoice and give thanks to Almighty God for the pouring out of His Spirit upon *all* people.

Those around us can see we have an undeniable *"hope."* We need to be ready for when they ask: *"What is it about you?"* Or *"Why are you always so happy?"* Share the gospel with them. Those who respond and receive *"the promise of the Father"* may thank you for your faithful testimony later.

Not everybody is ready to hear what we have to say. From New Testament times through to today these words from the book of Hebrews explain a lot:

2. *For unto us was the gospel preached, as well as unto them: but the word preached did not profit them, not being mixed with faith in them that heard it.*
— Hebrews 4:2

If people have no belief in God or the gospel we preach then what we say is of little perceived value to them.

Can we fire up even a spark of faith in them?

Have we stopped looking at the universe God created?

The Bible says we are *"without excuse"*:

> 20. *For the invisible things of him from the creation of the world are clearly seen, being understood by the things that are made, even his eternal power and Godhead; so that they are without excuse:*
> 21. *Because that, when they knew God, they glorified him not as God, neither were thankful; but became vain in their imaginations, and their foolish heart was darkened.*
> 22. *Professing themselves to be wise, they became fools,*
> — Romans 1:20–22

Professing ourselves to be wise, we are become as fools!

Have we stopped looking at the countless forms of life across what we call nature? Look at the variety and complexity. In the human body there is over 20,000 different protein-coding genes. Scientists estimate there could be 70,000 to 100,000 proteins in us. Where did they come from?

The possibility that even one of these proteins happens to exist by chance is exceeding remote. The probability is less than miniscule. The Word of God has this to say about people who have such imagined expectations:

> 1. *The fool hath said in his heart, There is no God. They are corrupt, they have done abominable works, there is none that doeth good.*
> — Psalms 14:1

Have we stopped wondering Who made our own senses?

Eyesight that can discern light and dark and a spectrum of beautiful colors with variations in shading. The ability of our brain to observe near and far objects and even estimate their speed and distance and recognise what and whom we see. Eyes to see God's glorious creation in all its splendour. Beautiful flowers and trees and landscapes, animals and birds and fish and insects, not to mention friends and family and those we hold dear.

Hearing ears that listen to everything from the faintest whisper to the loudest crash. Their connection to our brain helps us appreciate music and make sense of speech. We recognise voices and can associate what we hear with friend or foe. We delight in the chirping of birds, the splashing of fish and the call of sheep and cattle. I expect you have your own favourite sounds.

We have a nose that provides us with a sense of smell that can detect fragrances as well as the most acrid of odours. We can smell the freshness of air and the aroma of a beautiful meal. We delight in the scent of the variety of flowers and grasses and trees God has created and we breathe in and out the life giving air through our nose.

A tongue with taste receptors to help us enjoy the flavours of our favourite food. We can discern the freshness of what we taste, and can detect acidity and spice and the beauty of cream. We can also tell when these substances have turned sour or gone off and should not get consumed.

Temperature and pressure receptors in our skin provide us with a sense of touch and feel to help us detect a gossamer breeze through to the strongest blow? We can appreciate a lover's caress, a friendly hug, and a firm handshake. We can feel roughness and smoothness, and degrees of softness and firmness and hardness. We can feel the sharpness or bluntness of a cutting tool, and use our fingers and hands to work at an astonishing variety of fashion and industry.

Have people stopped looking up into the sky at night to consider the majesty of the God's handiwork in space? Billions of *galaxies* exist out there. NASA estimates there is 100 billion *stars* in our own galaxy, the Milky Way.

Will we stop, even for a moment to reconsider? What if the gospel is the truth? We claim it's true. The *"born again"* experience we have is undeniable.

I believe this knowledge and experience represents the utmost truth we can discover about life, the universe and all that we can discern.

We praise and thank God for preserving His Word for us to search and read and digest and understand through the *"promise of the Father"* that makes us *"born again"* and gives us Spiritual insight.

We can remind people that God says:

> 3. *Call unto me, and I will answer thee, and shew thee great and mighty things, which thou knowest not.*
> — Jeremiah 33:3

Jesus commanded His disciples and believers to *"wait for the promise of the Father."*

On the day of Pentecost 2,000 years ago they experienced the truth of His statements when they each received *"the gift of the Holy Ghost."*

When Jesus said: *"You must be born again,"* this is the experience He was pointing us to.

We implore everyone — please test Peter's words for yourself:

> 38. *Then Peter said unto them, Repent, and be baptized every one of you in the name of Jesus*

*Christ for the remission of sins, and ye shall
receive the gift of the Holy Ghost.*
*39. For the promise is unto you, and to your
children, and to all that are afar off, even as
many as the LORD our God shall call.*
— Acts 2:38–39

It's a three step process:

1. Repent

Turn aside from doing your own thing all the time.

Make a humble and honest approach towards God.

2. Get baptized

Do what God has asked us to do.

Go through the short process of water baptism.

It takes a little bit of humility.

It demonstrates our intentions are good.

The Word of God declares that all have sinned and
come short of the glory of God.

Jesus died to wash away our sins.

3. Receive God's Holy Spirit

Ask God for the promise of the Father.

Spend time talking to God with humility and sincerity.

The moment we receive the *"promise of the Father"* we
will start speaking in an unlearned tongue.

Do not get discouraged.

Jesus says:

> *7. Ask, and it shall be given you; seek, and ye
> shall find; knock, and it shall be opened unto
> you:*

8. *For every one that asketh receiveth; and he that seeketh findeth; and to him that knocketh it shall be opened.*
— Matthew 7:7–8

Before long we expect there will be a pleasant surprise.

Sharing our testimony with people need not get too complicated. We do not need to cover everything from Genesis to Revelation in one sitting. That will overwhelm people.

The person who shared the gospel with me listened to what I had picked up on in the daily newspapers scattered across our morning and afternoon tea tables at wotk, and he would say: *"In the church I attend people still get healed today by the power of God — it happens all the time."*

If I was complaining about war and strife in the world he would remind me that Jesus said: *"nation shall rise against nation, and kingdom against kingdom: and there shall be famines, and pestilences, and earthquakes, in divers places."* See: Matthew 24, verse 7.

When I responded and wanted to know more he would offer more information — telling me about the Holy Spirit experience. If I needed to get back to the work I was doing he would wait until we met again.

When should we go about preaching the gospel? This verse from 1st Peter, chapter 3, reminds us we should *"be ready always:"*

15. *But sanctify the Lord God in your hearts: and be ready always to give an answer to every man that asketh you a reason of the hope that is in you with meekness and fear:*
— 1 Peter 3:15

www.ingramcontent.com/pod-product-compliance
Lightning Source LLC
Chambersburg PA
CBHW071904020426
42331CB00010B/2670